MAKING A START IN
N GAUGE
RAILWAY MODELLING

MAKING A START IN
N GAUGE
RAILWAY MODELLING

Richard Bardsley

THE CROWOOD PRESS

First published in 2013 by
The Crowood Press Ltd
Ramsbury, Marlborough
Wiltshire SN8 2HR

enquiries@crowood.com

www.crowood.com

This impression 2023

British Library Cataloguing-in-Publication Data
A catalogue record for this book is available from the British Library.

ISBN 978 1 84797 556 0

Acknowledgements
Writing this second book was as much fun as the first. Once again, I could not have done it
without the help of family and friends. I'd like to thank: my wife Sharon Bardsley for further
encouragement; my father Stuart Bardsley for more proofing; my mother Margaret Bardsley for
buying me my first ever N gauge locomotive; Colin Whalley for lending me items to photograph.
For their superb photos, I thank Fred Hempsall (Lincoln and District Model Railway Club) and
Grahame Hedges. For letting me photograph their layouts, I thank: Ray Slack; the Northants &
Cambs Area Group of the N Gauge Society; John Spence; the Leamington & Warwick Model
Railway Society; the Warrington Model Railway Club; Mike Le Marie; the Wyre Forest Model
Railway Club; Pete Latham. Finally, thanks are due to the manufacturers large and small for
supporting N gauge.

Disclaimer
The author and the publisher do not accept any responsibility in any manner whatsoever for any
error or omission, or any loss, damage, injury, adverse outcome, or liability of any kind incurred
as a result of the use of any of the information contained in this book, or reliance upon it.

Previous page: 'Burnham-on-Sea' by Alistair Knox represents a bustling seaside resort in the
pre-war days of the LMS. There are lots of fascinating little details that bring this scene to life
such as people, street lamps, road vehicles and a telephone box.

Typeset and designed by D & N Publishing, Baydon, Wiltshire
Printed and bound by CPI Group (UK) Ltd, Croydon CR0 4YY

CONTENTS

'Melton Mowbray (North)' is an exhibition layout by John Spence and Steve Weston that faithfully represents a real place. The additional space that is available in N gauge gives this scene more depth than would be possible in the same space in a larger scale thus enhancing its realism.

INTRODUCTION

If you had a train set when you were young, or perhaps your children had a train set, it's almost certain that it was in OO gauge, which has been the most popular commercial scale. It's equally likely that when you put the basic oval of track together, it did not fit on the dining-room table, and you probably ended up on the floor. Despite having fun, how often did you say to yourself, 'I wish it was a bit smaller'? In this book, you will see that the trains are a bit smaller, that they will fit on to the dining table and that you have discovered the marvellous world of N gauge.

There are more reasons for choosing N gauge than just being short of space. While the height and width in N gauge are half the size of OO gauge, the actual area is one-quarter of that required for OO gauge. So if you want to build a layout with sweeping viaducts crossing huge valleys, you will get a much greater visual impact in N gauge. In the real world, the landscape came before the railway; without room to let the scenery breathe, it can simply look like an afterthought. Even the urban environment looks better in N gauge, as you can develop streets, shops and factories. It's all about setting the scene and then setting the railway into the scene. There are many railway modellers with significant areas of space available who still choose N gauge for this reason.

Do not think that by choosing N gauge you have in some way compromised your desire to build a realistic model railway by choosing a smaller scale. The opposite is true – you have made a deliberate decision to choose a modelling scale that best suits what you want to achieve. Many modellers in larger scales have to compromise in terms of the length of their trains. A full-length, main-line express train will often be ten coaches; the larger the scale, the more of those carriages you have to surrender to fit it on to your layout. In a modest-sized room for your layout, N gauge will let you have the whole train without any compromises.

If you are new to the model railway hobby, or just to N gauge itself, you may not know where to begin. There are lots of questions, and without easily understood answers, you may be unsure about how to get

N gauge offers the chance for stunning scenic vistas, while also allowing real places to be modelled, virtually to scale, such as this view of Bodmin in Great Western Railway days as modelled by Ray Slack and Ian Hibbert.

going. Building a rewarding N gauge model railway is just a series of bite-sized steps performed in a logical manner. The starting point is a bit of design – where will you put your model railway, what type of layout will you build and which prototype will you choose? When you know what you want, you can draw a track plan that is a blueprint for the layout you are going to build. Construction itself starts with the foundation of baseboards. Then the excitement really starts as you are ready to lay and ballast the track. Once this is done, you can add wiring and controls, and you can actually play trains.

It is now possible to achieve a stunning level of realism when modelling in N gauge thanks to the quality of the models available and the space to let them become part of a landscape. This fact is superbly illustrated on Horseley Fields by the Northants & Cambs Area Group of the N Gauge Society.

To run some trains you will need rolling stock, and with this you will need to choose a coupling system for the way in which you will operate the layout. Once everything is working, you can construct the layout's scenic setting, starting with the immediate railway infrastructure, such as stations, and then the wider scenery of fields and hills or houses and factories. Finally, you can add the many little details that really bring a layout to life.

There has never been a better time to make a model railway layout in N gauge and it just keeps getting better. The last ten years have seen not just a resurgence in its popularity, but an explosion of new products and an astonishing improvement in standards. Super-detailed, powerful models of even the smallest prototype locomotives are now taken for granted; just a decade ago, no one would have dreamt that they would be possible. There are many reasons for this, such as improvements in manufacturing technology, and cheaper and greater production capability by using factories in the Far East. Above all, manufacturers need to see a demand before they invest millions of pounds – that demand is there, and their faith in the increasing N gauge market has been rewarded.

The increased interest in N gauge is in respect of models of the railways of Britain. Models of Continental and American prototypes in N gauge were, for so many years, far more advanced than most of what British manufacturers could offer. The benchmark for a superb model was referred to as matching the 'Continental standard'. That British N gauge models have equalled, and in some cases exceeded, the Continental standard in little more than a decade is a sign of just how far British N gauge modelling has come.

The hobby of model railways is a brilliant one, and many thousands of people enjoy what it has to offer every day. More and more of those modellers are becoming N gauge modellers. Whether you are new to the model railway hobby or an established railway modeller looking to change to N gauge, this book will tell you everything you need to know about how to make a start in N gauge.

CHAPTER ONE

WHAT IS N GAUGE?

If you are new to the model railway hobby, even if you've already been interested for a while, the phrases and terminology can be a little confusing at first. Every walk of life has its jargon, a secret language that can be perceived by the outsider as only understandable to the insider. Model railways has its fair share of terms; however, every term has an explanation, so this chapter looks at everything you need to know to understand N gauge before you get started.

Some aspects have more than one name for the same thing, such as scale and gauge; not surprisingly, British modellers define things slightly differently to everyone else. This is for historical reasons, so it's worth looking at a little bit of history to see how N gauge evolved to become what it is today. Broadly speaking, 'N gauge' is simply a label that defines the size of the model; that size has many advantages and a few disadvantages when compared to other sizes of models, and it is important to look at the pros and cons in relation to what you want to do with a model railway.

SCALE AND GAUGE EXPLAINED

There are two key things that define the size of any model railway and they are its scale and its gauge. All models are defined by a scale, not just model railways. If you are modelling planes, trains or automobiles, they are also made to scale in just the same way. Sometimes the scale of an aeroplane or ship model is virtually the same as N gauge, which is helpful if you want to model a port or an airport. Gauge as a definition of the model is something that is unique to model railways.

If there were always strict and consistent rules of miniaturization, then the relationship between scale and gauge would always be the same and the one would always relate exactly to the other. In reality, it's not quite that simple, which is the fault of history. With hindsight, if you were to define N gauge from scratch today, it's certain that it would be a little different from what it actually is.

If you find the concepts of scale a little hard to get to grips with, a Peco 'British N Scale' ruler will help. It has the two main scale definitions printed on it (the ratio of 1:148 and the scale of $2\frac{1}{16}$mm to the foot) and some useful information for Peco's own products, such as track centres. Its main advantage is that the ruler's units are in 'scale feet'. The real shock-absorbing open wagons had a wheelbase (distance between wheel centres) of 10ft and you can see on the model that this has been correctly scaled down to N gauge.

SCALE

The scale of a model is simply how many times smaller it is than the real prototype that it represents. It is written as a ratio. If you were to model something as half the size that it actually is, then the scale would be 1:2 (if you were to read this out loud, you would say 'one to two'). Sometimes, when writing the scale, the colon is replaced with a forward slash, so 1:2 might be written 1/2, which is actually a fraction (the model is half the size of the real thing).

Writing a scale as 1:2 is a very clear and simple definition of how small your model is; you can think of it as saying that every one unit of measure on the model is equivalent to two units of measure on the real thing. N gauge is a ratio of 1:148, therefore N gauge model trains are 148 times smaller than they are in real life. So 148 real inches (that's just over 12ft or 3,657mm) requires just 1 inch (25mm) in N gauge.

When scale is written as a ratio like this, it's nice and simple and really easy to visualize. Its simplicity lies in the fact that the units of measure are the same – one unit of measure on the model equates to 148 units of measure on the real thing. So the next definition of N gauge might seem a little odd, since it mixes different units of measure. You will often see N gauge defined as 2mm:1ft, which is read out loud as 'two millimetres to the foot'. So every 2mm on the model represents 1ft on the real thing. As long as you measure the model in metric measurements and the prototype in imperial measurements, you will be all right. It's a useful definition of scale because, rather than dividing all real dimensions by 148 to get the model dimension, all you have to do is multiply both sides of the ratio by the same factor. For example, 20mm in N Gauge is 10ft in real life.

Those of you who are comfortable with maths and have followed the example above with a calculator will notice that the sums do not quite add up. If you divide 10ft by 148 you get $^{13}/_{16}$th of an inch, which is 20.6mm and not 20mm. You will often see N gauge referred to in books and magazines as 2mm:1ft but that's not quite correct. It is actually 2.0625mm:1ft, more commonly written as 2$^1/_{16}$mm:1ft or 'two and one-sixteenth millimetres to one foot'. N gauge is a modelling scale that is unique to Britain for historical

reasons (and not just because the British like to be different to the rest of the world).

GAUGE

Having defined N gauge in terms of scale, how do we define it in terms of gauge? A dictionary definition of gauge is 'the distance between pairs of rails or between opposite wheels'. It's as simple as that, and reveals what the 'N' of N gauge stands for – it is an abbreviation of 'nine' and the unit of measure is metric. N gauge actually means 'nine-millimetre gauge'. The standard gauge of real railways is 4ft 8½in; however, dividing this by 148 and converting from imperial to metric is not 9mm but instead equals 9.65mm. Once again, historical reasons make British models slightly different.

The use of the term 'N gauge' is a peculiarly British thing. The rest of the world refers to 'N scale'. Their term is actually a slight misnomer, since it suggests '9mm scale' when it is clearly nowhere near a scale ratio of 9mm to anything. N scale really means 'a scale using 9mm gauge track' or '9mm gauge track scale'. It's a curious development of what was the established naming convention.

At one time, O scale (or O gauge in Britain) was the dominant scale (a scale ratio of 1:48, or 7mm:1ft). The next logical development was models that were half the size of O scale and indeed it became HO scale ('Half O scale', which is a scale ratio of 1:87 or 3.5mm:1ft). N scale might have become HHO (Half HO) but a scale of 1.75mm:1ft might well have pushed the limits of miniaturization at the time. So instead, there was a break with tradition and N scale it became. The British use of 'N gauge' as a label is perhaps a more accurate one than 'N scale'. Many modellers just refer to working in 'N' without feeling the need to add 'gauge' or 'scale'. When something can be referred to by just a single letter and yet everyone understands what it is, that's a very strong brand association indeed.

BRITAIN VERSUS THE REST OF THE WORLD

Although it may be confusing for Britain to refer to 'N gauge' and the rest of the world to refer to 'N scale', it's more than a case of the British being obstinately different; there is actually a subtle difference between N gauge and N scale. British N gauge is a scale ratio of 1:148, but most of the rest of the world works to a scale ratio of 1:160. This results in models that are fractionally smaller than their British counterparts.

To the casual observer, this difference between the scale ratio of N gauge and N scale will be hard to detect. Only if you were to place two models (one made to N gauge and the other made to N scale) of the same prototype side by side would you really be able to spot the difference. In some cases it's impossible to tell a difference, but it depends what you are looking at. Buildings are a good example, since they come in all shapes and sizes; how would you tell if a window frame was N gauge or N scale? Model people are also interchangeable between N gauge and N scale since in real life, people come in all shapes and sizes so a subtle difference will not be detectable.

Some international wagons travel from Britain to the Continent and vice versa. Mixing models from N gauge and N scale in the same train to represent this (either side of the Channel) may still work. The difference only tends to become noticeable on the longer wagons, but as wagons, like people, come in all shapes and sizes, you would probably need to have a very keen eye for the prototype to detect the discrepancy.

One area where the difference in scale tends to be noticeable is with road vehicles. If you place an N gauge lorry next to its Continental counterpart in N scale, even if they represent different lorries, the chances are that you will notice the disparity. However, if you use N scale road vehicles on an N gauge layout, it is likely that you will not notice a difference, even though they are actually slightly small for N gauge. The key concept here is to be consistent with where you source your road vehicles from, or to keep them obviously separated on the layout.

N scale, with its scale ratio of 1:160, is the de facto standard across the Continent and America. There, as in Britain, it is the second most popular model railway scale (after HO, or OO gauge in Britain). The one country where N scale is the most popular commercial scale is Japan. This fact is possibly explained by Japan being a country where the scarcity of living space means that a smaller scale is the only practical one for most people. Just to be different once again, the Japanese model to a scale ratio of 1:150, which is barely distinguish from the British 1:148. This means that British and Japanese models are fully interchangeable without any worries about slight scale discrepancies. The huge range of Japanese collectible road vehicles is immensely popular with British modellers, not least because the Japanese also drive on the left.

N gauge and N scale are actually different, even though they are often used by modellers interchangeably. On the left is a North American GP7, while on the right is a British Class 26. Both are small-size, four-axle mixed traffic locomotives, yet the GP7 looks noticeably larger than its British cousin; however, the American model is actually smaller than the British one because the former is to a scale of 1:160 (N scale), while the latter is to a scale of 1:148 (N gauge).

2mm FINE SCALE

Given that British N gauge has ended up as a series of compromises, it's not surprising that some modellers seek to sort out what they perceive to be a bit of a mess of standards and inaccuracies. Modellers using 2mm fine scale, model to a scale ratio of exactly 2mm:1ft rather than N gauge's 2$\frac{1}{16}$mm:1ft. They also seek to get the track gauge right and work to a gauge of 9.42mm.

To model in 2mm fine scale, as opposed to N gauge, requires a greater level of modelling skill. Track tends to be hand-built rather than commercially produced. There is a lot of scratch building and conversion of N gauge models, such as replacing chassis and wheels for ones with finer standards and greater levels of detail.

In the past, when the commercial output for N gauge could look a little toy-like, a layout built to 2mm fine-scale standards really looked superb and stood out from the crowd. Now that ready-to-run products have improved so much, they have closed what was once a huge gap in fidelity. Models in 2mm fine scale still have the edge, so it's still worth checking out if you're striving for one hundred per cent accuracy and realism.

COMPARING N GAUGE WITH OTHER SCALES

The three main commercial scales in Britain are O gauge, OO gauge and N gauge. This also holds true across the world (O scale, HO scale and N scale). There are plenty of other scales, though you will probably find that you need more experienced modelling skills to exploit them, as they offer few, if any, ready-to-run models. Each of the three main scales has something going for it, yet each will have its drawbacks.

The most popular commercial scale is still OO gauge, a scale of 4mm:1ft. This puts it in the middle of the commercially popular scales in terms of size. There is a big range of ready-to-run rolling stock and supporting scenic items available. The latest ready-to-run locos have the fidelity and detail previously only seen in O gauge, yet the scale takes up half the space.

You still need a room-sized space if you want even a modest oval-shaped layout.

The largest of the commercial scales is O gauge, which is a scale of 7mm:1ft. Although ready-to-run models are becoming increasingly available, it is still largely a kit-builder's scale, and significantly more expensive. Compared to N gauge, O gauge is huge, which limits you to very small layouts at home.

As a rule of thumb, N gauge requires half the length that you would need in OO gauge. This is an important consideration if you want a layout that will run long trains. N gauge also requires only one-quarter of the surface area when compared to OO gauge.

A LITTLE BIT OF HISTORY

N gauge is the second most popular railway modelling scale in the world. It may still have a way to go to challenge the dominance of OO gauge, but the improvements in N gauge models over the last decade have seen it advance far more than at any time previous to that. This was not always the case; indeed, there was a time when N gauge did not even exist.

Times and fashions change in the model railway hobby, as they do in anything. The only constant has been a greater public demand for commercially produced models than modellers were prepared to make for themselves. The potential popularity of a new scale attracts the interest of the entrepreneurial manufacturers; this results in the commercialization of a scale but does not guarantee its success. The only consistent trend has been to make the models smaller and smaller.

In the beginning, gauge 1 (1:32 or 10mm:1ft) was dominant. It's a massive scale for model railways, bordering on being miniature railway engineering. Popularity then passed to O gauge; that seems big to us now, but it must have seemed small to those for whom gauge 1 was the norm. O gauge remained the new dominant scale until the ability to commercially manufacture even smaller models (in OO gauge) virtually wiped out interest in O gauge (though it has since seen a healthy resurgence in popularity). N gauge has similarly challenged OO gauge over the last fifty years. It has never come close to becoming the

The three main commercial scales are shown here for comparison; from left to right are models in O gauge, OO gauge and N gauge of the same wagon – a British Railways Grampus ballast wagon.

dominant scale until now, where its market position gets ever closer to being a serious rival.

At a diminutive scale ratio of 1.4mm:1ft, Z gauge was the smallest commercial scale (though the models are usually of North American or Continental prototypes), until the recent introduction of the positively microscopic T scale (a scale ratio of 1:450). These scales have enough interest to make them commercial, but perhaps they are just too small to become really popular. It is possible that N gauge is about as small as most people are practically prepared to go.

Despite being a globally recognized and popular railway modelling scale, the roots of N gauge and N scale can be traced back to Britain. The commercial beginnings started in the 1950s with non-motorized diecast locomotives and rolling stock produced by Lone Star. As these were smaller than OO gauge, the fledgling scale was marketed as treble O (sometimes written as OOO). The Lone Star products had to be pushed along preformed sections of cast track of approximately 9mm gauge. In 1959, motorized products (branded as Treble-O-Lectric) became available, running on track with plastic sleepers to electrically isolate the two running rails.

The lead now switched to Germany, with Arnold Rapido producing an electric train system similar to the Lone Star product and also using 9mm gauge

track. Initially, a scale of 1:152 was used until the more accurate 1:160 was adopted. The Arnold products were followed by ones from Minitrix, Fleischmann and Rivarossi. Some of these companies made British prototype models in N gauge, though they were just minor sidelines to their main production of Continental and American models.

It is at this point, and possibly because of a lack of real focus from the Continental manufacturers, that the curious discrepancies of N gauge occurred with its unique scale ratio of 1:148. It was all down to the size of the real railways and another use for the word 'gauge'. All railways, both real and model, have a defined track gauge, but real railways have a further set of definitions, which are also referred to as the 'loading gauge'. These dimensions are basically the maximum height and width permissible for rolling stock to ensure that it does not foul lineside structures, such as bridges and platforms. It also ensures that anything loaded into an open wagon does not collide with a bridge (hence 'loading' gauge). Rolling stock that is within these dimensions is said to be 'within gauge'.

The problem was that the loading gauge in Britain was significantly less generous than that in the Continent and America. Locomotives abroad tended to be physically bigger. The smallest electric motors available for models during the 1960s were small enough to fit into models of Continental and American prototypes

This is a model by Minitrix (branded as Hornby Minitrix) of an Ivatt 2-6-0 locomotive. At first glance, it looks like the prototype, especially the distinctive tender; however, the locomotive chassis is from a German prototype, most obviously around the cylinders. The cab, firebox and boiler have also been compromised to accommodate the motor. Despite this, these models were always popular, not least because of the superb reliability and haulage power of the chassis manufactured on the Continent.

at a scale of 1:160. Prototype British locomotives were physically smaller and the electric motors would not fit. The manufacturers' answer was to make the British models slightly bigger until the electric motors would fit. A scale of 1:148 did the job and it has become the standard scale for N gauge ever since. Unfortunately, these manufacturers retained their 1:160 scale track with its 9mm gauge. The result is that British models run on track that is actually slightly narrower than it would be if it had been scaled down at exactly 1:148.

The Italian manufacturer Lima produced a small range of N gauge items in the early 1970s. Some of these were actually quite good models but they were let down by being noticeably under scale (at 1:160) and sometimes running on a very basic chassis. The wheels that Lima used were particularly over-scale in terms of flanges and treads (the Italian origins perhaps giving rise to them being described as 'pizza cutters').

The German company Minitrix (sold in the UK as Hornby Minitrix) produced a series of British steam and diesel locomotives, though somewhat adjusted in order to use existing chassis that were actually designed for Continental locomotives. Some of these models had only a passing resemblance to what they

The Italian manufacturer Lima produced a number of good-quality N gauge models during the 1970s, such as this GWR inside-framed Siphon G milk-churn carrying wagon. However, at Continental 1:160 scale, it appears a little under scale when used with 1:148 models, while the bogies and wheels are a little rudimentary.

It's hard to tell that over thirty years separate these two models of MGR hopper wagons. The Minitrix model on the right looks just as good as the recently introduced Peco model on the left. Only the slightly finer moulding of the chassis detail gives the modern Peco model the edge.

were supposed to represent, but their Continental chassis gave them superb haulage power and reliability. Their performance has meant that these models have remained popular with modellers until only recently, with the introduction of new and improved models. One area where Minitrix were famously ahead of their time was with the production of a model Merry-Go-Round (MGR) hopper wagon. Until the recent introduction of newer models by both Peco and Graham Farish by Bachmann, the Minitrix MGR wagons were able to maintain exorbitant second-hand prices.

In the early 1970s, the British manufacturer Graham Farish spotted an opening in the N gauge market for models of British prototypes. The initial range proved to be popular and slowly expanded over the next thirty years to include many locomotives, coaches and wagons, all produced at the Poole factory in Dorset. Production transferred to China in 2000 when the company was sold to Bachmann Industries Europe Ltd. Models continue to be sold under the Graham Farish banner as 'Graham Farish by Bachmann' and are referred to by either or both of these company names (as well as just Farish, Grafar or GF).

Almost in parallel with Graham Farish, Peco (Pritchard Patent Products Ltd) developed a range of track, wagons and scenic accessories that have proven to be a firm foundation for British N gauge

The GWR 94xx pannier tank locomotive is probably synonymous with the early years of model production from Graham Farish. This well-used example is thirty years old and still going strong.

TOP: The purchase of the Graham Farish brand by Bachmann in 2000 saw production moved from Britain to China. There was a protracted delay in setting up the new production lines, but it was worth the wait, as some subtle upgrades were immediately made. The Chinese-produced 57xx 0-6-0PT on the left has had a chassis upgrade compared to the Poole factory-produced model on the right – the wheels are to a finer profile and blackened, as are the coupling rods.

ABOVE: The testament to the quality and fidelity of Peco's model of the LMS Jubilee 4-6-0 tender locomotive is the inflated second-hand prices that they were able to maintain for thirty years, until the recent introduction of a new model from Graham Farish by Bachmann. By placing the electric motor in the tender, the designers were able to model the locomotive's boiler correctly, without having to compromise it to fit in a motor.

modellers. There was initially just one foray into producing a locomotive model (in conjunction with Rivarossi), which was the 'Jubilee', whose quality was to be unrivalled in N gauge for nearly thirty years. Peco track is sold around the world (being 9mm gauge, it is to a scale of 1:160 and thus perfectly suitable for Continental and American layouts). All Peco products are still made in Britain.

The next significant entrant to the British prototype scene was the arrival of Dapol in 2004 with a series of locomotives that showed a significant improvement in fidelity over anything that had been previously produced for the British market. They were initially manufactured in Britain before expanding to use the larger-scale production facilities offered in the Far East. Dapol are credited with introducing many of the innovations that we now take for granted in N gauge, such as bi-directional lighting on diesel locomotives.

Like Graham Farish over thirty years previously, Dapol spotted a gap in the market, and their entry into the market began the rapid improvement in production standards and fidelity that has enhanced N gauge over the last decade. This improvement has proceeded at a phenomenal rate and hardly a month passes without a new locomotive being released. Compare this to

The competitive race to improve manufacturing fidelity started in 2004 when Dapol released their first models in N gauge. This is a first-production run GWR 14xx 0-4-2T loco with matching auto-coach. The feature that gives it away as one of the first batch of models is that the locomotive's wheel rims and coupling rods are shiny. All subsequent models featured blackened wheels and rods, which are more prototypical – an example of the constant improvement now seen from manufacturers.

twenty years ago when N gauge modellers were lucky to get one new locomotive a year.

THE ADVANTAGES OF N GAUGE

It goes without saying that the advantage of N gauge is that it takes up less space. It's smaller than OO gauge so, of course, it needs a smaller amount of space. Do not just choose N gauge because it takes up less room, as there are a number of other good reasons to select N gauge, which are variations on a theme, in that they are space-related; but one or all of

these reasons could be vital to what you want to achieve with your model railway.

MORE RAILWAY IN LESS SPACE

Most modellers will tell you that they'd like a bit more space for their model railway, even those with large lofts or rooms at their disposal. Railway modellers are like empire builders – they always want to expand. If you only have a limited space available, such as part of a room or a small garden shed, it's obvious that a smaller scale will allow you to get more railway into that space.

One locomotive above all others shows how far N gauge has now progressed. The model on the left is an original Graham Farish Class 08 0-6-0 diesel shunter from the early 1970s. The same locomotive on the right is a brand-new Graham Farish by Bachmann model, which now has the correct outside frame cranks, blackened wheels, separate handrails, buffer beam detail (including coupling hooks), radiator filler pipes, cab glazing, sand boxes and sanding pipes.

N gauge is half the length of OO gauge and so it will take up one-quarter of the space. That means that you can have four times as much railway in the same space if you use N gauge instead of OO gauge. If you want an oval-type layout, so that you can just sit and watch the trains go by, you can even manage this on a single baseboard that will fit on the dining table.

Don't just think in terms of cramming four times as much railway into the same space. Having that much more space by using N gauge means that you have the space to let the layout breathe. Instead of a cramped layout in OO gauge, consider exactly the same track plan in N gauge. Using OO gauge may mean having to have shorter sidings and platforms to get it all in. Using N gauge instead means that the sidings and platforms can be of a prototypical length. The extra space means that you will have to make

fewer (if any) compromises in your track plan; this is especially important if you are trying to recreate an actual location. In addition, the extra space gives you more opportunity to set the layout in the landscape.

SCENERY – A LAYOUT IN THE LANDSCAPE

The model railway hobby means different things to different people. Thankfully, this variety of interest makes for a wonderfully diverse hobby. Some modellers focus on operation and don't worry too much about the scenery beyond the railway boundary fence. Others like to place the railway into a panorama, a bit like creating a three-dimensional landscape painting. To do this you need space, even if you just want to thread a single railway line through the hills and valleys.

John Spence and Steve Weston have built an amazing N gauge layout depicting Melton Mowbray (North). In order to model an actual location, they have used the space-saving capabilities of N gauge to avoid having to compromise. Using the same baseboard area in OO gauge, there would have been much less opportunity to model the area surrounding the station that gives the location its character.

In the real world, the landscape came first; engineers surveyed it and drove a railway through it. As railway modellers, we tend to focus on the railway and then wrap the scenery around it, almost as an afterthought. Using N gauge means that you can consider the space for your layout as a landscape first and add the railway in afterwards. There are many classic locations, such as the Scottish Highlands or the Settle to Carlisle line, that really need enough space around the model railway to do justice to the impressive backdrop.

It's not just rural landscapes that will benefit from having space to model them; the urban environment has lots of houses and factories that can be modelled to give an atmospheric setting for your trains. Choosing N gauge to model such scenic vistas will give you the chance to have the best of both worlds – brilliant scenery and scale-length trains.

VERY LONG TRAINS

If you are modelling a branch line in a rural backwater, you don't need to worry too much about train length. If you want all the excitement of full-length express trains or heavy freights, then you need to consider how to cater for very long trains. Railways are long, thin things, and so are very long trains. N gauge takes up half the length of OO gauge, so that means that you can have trains that are twice as long in the same space.

When viewed from a distance, real trains tend to get lost in the surrounding landscape. N gauge gives you the opportunity to build enough scenery on either side of the railway line to achieve this, as here with a view of Lincoln and District Model Railway Club's layout Peakdale. Photo: Fred Hempsall

Scenery does not have to be about trees and hills; the urban environment offers just as many scenic challenges. This astonishing townscape of terraced houses for the workers at the factory in the distance was created by the Leamington & Warwick Model Railway Society on their exhibition layout called Meacham.

This is a block train working, 1950s style. The Class 24 hauled oil train has twenty wagons; this is probably shorter than the actual train ran in real life, but it still looks impressive. Using N gauge means that this very long train does not take over the surrounding landscape – everything looks to be in proportion. This outstanding scene depicting an actual train at an actual location was created by the Warrington Model Railway Club on their exhibition layout Glazebrook.

Railway companies have always liked running long trains, just as much in the steam era as with today's modern railway. Such trains are more efficient as they carry more passengers or freight for the same locomotive and staff. The limiting factors tend to be the length of some of the infrastructure, such as platforms and loops. Mainline express trains were often loaded to ten or twelve bogie coaches in the steam era; a High Speed Train (HST) has at least eight Mark 3 coaches, each 70ft (21.3m) long. Some steam-era coal trains would run to one hundred wagons, while a standard Merry-Go-Round (MGR) coal train consisted of thirty-six long-wheelbase hopper wagons. The latest so-called 'block trains' are even longer.

Even in N gauge, you may have to resort to a little bit of selective compression, running twenty-four MGR hoppers instead of thirty-six, or nine coaches instead of twelve. A slight reduction still retains the essential essence of the real train. Consider that in

OO gauge in the same space, you may only have room for your express train to have five coaches; in that case, it's more like a stopping train than an express. A severely truncated express train won't look the part, especially when it's speeding round tight curves.

EASIER CURVES

Traditionally, the minimum radius in OO gauge is 18in (457mm), while in N gauge it is 9in (229mm). Most rolling stock will just about run round these minimum radii in either scale. However, some manufacturers making a modern generation of model locomotives are publishing a minimum radius greater than these traditional values. Just like real trains, your model trains will generate greater friction on the track as they pass into the curves. Modern locomotive models are very powerful and the rolling stock is very free-wheeling, but it is something to be aware of – you don't want to see your train stalling, with wheels spinning, halfway around a curve.

The main problem with tight curves is that they look unrealistic. It is only really noticeable with bogie rolling stock. Short-wheelbase wagons that are typical of the steam era look fine on a tight curve. The main problem with coaches is their length. A British Rail Mark 3 coach is 70ft (21.3m) long – a model of such a vehicle will therefore overhang the inner face of a tight curve quite considerably.

If you model in OO gauge, you may only have room for 18in (46cm) curves. You can use the same radius in the same space with N gauge; an 18in-radius curve in N gauge is now twice the minimum radius. While this still scales out as a lot less than the real minimum radius for trains, the curves will not look as tight as they do in OO gauge. The overhang of bogie stock will be much reduced, which means that trains will look more realistic, especially at express train speeds.

ARE THERE ANY DISADVANTAGES TO N GAUGE?

It would be less than honest not to point out a few potential disadvantages with N gauge compared to the other scales. It's only fair to give a balanced view, although the many advantages of N gauge do far out-weigh a few possible shortcomings. Some modellers might be put off by the small size, the level of detail or the couplers.

SIZE

Some modellers look at N gauge and think that it is literally too small for them to get to grips with. The smaller size of N gauge is its chief advantage, yet for some it is seen as its main disadvantage. As fingers and eyes age, things become a little harder to grasp and to see. There are things that can help, like an illuminated magnifier or a re-railer to help you get rolling stock onto the track. Consider that a track pin in OO gauge is just as small as one in N gauge (they are the same, of course).

While O gauge models are much bigger, some of the kits can have the smallest parts imaginable. So even the larger modelling scales can, at times, be 'too small'. Therefore, how big does something have to be before it's no longer considered to be too small? N gauge is certainly not too small to be practical for most people. After all, the manufacturers have now solved the problems of including into small-scale modelling similar levels of detail as seen in large-scale modelling.

DETAIL AND FIDELITY

As models get smaller in terms of scale, the details that they contain become smaller until they cannot be seen any more. Worse, there is a risk that in try-ing to incorporate a detail, it has to be made slightly over-scale in order for it to be seen or for it to be strong enough to withstand manufacture and

If you are unsure about your ability to get small N gauge wheels on to the track, then you can use a re-railer. This cheap and simple bit of plastic is placed on the track when you need to get rolling stock onto the layout. Just put the rolling stock on to the re-railer and let gravity do the rest; the guides at the end will direct the wheels on to the track. It is long enough to take a coach or a locomotive (the latter will have to be pushed on to the track as the motor locks the wheels).

subsequent handling. If you want models where you can see and count every last rivet with the naked eye, then you should probably consider O gauge.

Some of the early attempts at commercial British N gauge models did look a little bit toy-like. Those from the Continental manufacturers were often a British prototype body mated to a Continental prototype chassis. With the notable exception of Peco's Jubilee, home-grown products could look a little crude, having under-scale wheels with over-scale flanges.

Modern manufacturing has come a long way since those early days, particularly in the last decade. Laser scanning of real locomotives can render all the subtle curves and shapes perfectly, while Computer Aided Design (CAD) means that models can be designed and perfected 'virtually' before any tooling is cut. The tooling itself is produced by computer to be accurate and reliable. Quite frankly, it's now difficult to tell which model is OO gauge and which is N gauge unless you look at the couplers.

N GAUGE COUPLINGS

The origins of British N gauge were shaped by the Continental manufacturers, leading to a unique scale ratio of 1:148 and track that's slightly narrower in gauge than it should be. Similarly, the so-called 'standard N gauge coupler' owes its origins to the early Arnold Rapido products. Indeed, the standard N gauge coupler is often referred to as the 'Rapido' coupler.

There's no getting away from the fact that it's a big chunk of black plastic on the ends of all items of rolling stock. It's not too bad on the end of a long coach, but on the end of a locomotive or a small wagon it can stick out like a sore thumb. In its favour, the coupling is robust, couples easily, can be uncoupled remotely and is made to a universal standard; no matter who has made the model, it will couple to other manufacturer's models.

Real couplings on real trains are either a three-link chain or a knuckle coupler. Chain-type couplings are tricky to use in O gauge, very fiddly in OO gauge and probably impossible in N gauge. Knuckle couplers are popular in America; as modelled, they are still over-scale but at least they look and operate like the real thing. The standard OO gauge coupling is the tension-lock coupler. While modern models now use 'slim line' tension-lock couplers, they are no less ugly, obtrusive or unrealistic in OO gauge than the standard N gauge coupler. No matter what you use for a coupler on models, if it is to be robust and usable, it is inevitable that it will have some drawbacks, in any scale, not just N gauge.

There are limits to the level of detail that can be incorporated into a OO gauge model, let alone an N gauge one. This is the same Class 03 locomotive from Bachmann, one in each scale. All the key details, such as handrails, are present in both models. Such is the quality of N gauge manufacturing today that, other than the physical size, it's hard to tell them apart.

THE N GAUGE SOCIETY

The pastime of railway modelling does not have to be a solitary affair if you do not want it to be. You may be fortunate to have a model railway club in your area. If you are a beginner, do not think that you will be unwelcome amongst its experienced members. The opposite will be true, as most model railway clubs are always on the lookout for new members. They love nothing better than to pass on their accumulated wisdom to anyone who needs help getting started.

The model railway hobby is also blessed with numerous societies devoted to particular aspects of modelling railways. It is perhaps no surprise to find a society that is dedicated to N gauge. For anyone who is modelling in N gauge, a subscription to the N Gauge Society is a worthwhile investment. It was formed in 1967 with the aim of promoting and developing modelling in N gauge. Membership is mostly based in Britain but there are members all around the world.

Since its formation, the N Gauge Society has developed and acquired a diverse range of wagon kits that are only available to members. This is now the single biggest offering of wagon kits in N gauge, as well as a growing range of ready-to-run wagons and coaches. Yet the N Gauge Society offers more than just products. Crucially for beginners, it is able to offer help and advice, especially if you are able to join one of the many active area groups throughout the country. Even if you cannot get to an area group, there is a helpline that puts you in touch with other members who can solve your problems. Ideas and inspiration are just as important and the bi-monthly N Gauge Society Journal contains layouts, product reviews and 'how to' articles that demonstrate what can be achieved with N gauge at all skill levels.

Membership of the N Gauge Society has many advantages, such as putting you in contact with thousands of other N gauge modellers. A substantial benefit is access to the biggest range of N gauge wagon kits, as well as some exclusive ready-to-run wagons and coaches. This selection barely scratches the surface of what is available and as can be seen, it covers every single modelling era.

CHAPTER TWO

DESIGNING AN N GAUGE LAYOUT

You can just let a layout evolve as you go along, if that's the way that you want to do it; however, a little bit of design will go a long way, mainly by helping you to avoid mistakes further down the line. By thinking about what sort of layout you want to achieve before you start, you will make sure that you end up with what you want and not be disappointed. Much of the design process for a layout is the same regardless of the scale you are working with, although there are one or two considerations specific to N gauge layouts.

You start by identifying where your layout will live, then the type of layout you want and the prototype it will represent. Make sure to include a fiddle yard to represent the rest of the railway network. Distil all your ideas for the layout so that you can draw out your plan and refine it, until finally you have a design that you can't wait to construct.

A ROOM FOR YOUR LAYOUT

There are a number of traditional places where you can put a model railway layout, and a few more unusual ones besides that. As N gauge is smaller than the other commercially available scales, space is less of a problem. Where you might have struggled to get an OO gauge layout into a typical 6ft × 8ft (1,829mm × 2,438mm) garden shed, with N gauge it will be easy. If you have a decent-sized space available, N gauge offers you the freedom to use your imagination to fill that space. If you have limited space, or must have a portable layout, N gauge will make it easier and allow you to have the railway you want in less space, more so than the larger scales.

A look at the traditional locations for a layout starts with room-sized spaces. A spare bedroom is the most luxurious of potential accommodation, as it's easily accessible within the house and offers a permanent home for a layout. No matter what size the room, it will easily have space for an N gauge layout. Even if the room has a dual purpose, such as a home office or a guest bedroom, an N gauge layout can be made to fit alongside. One option is a shelf layout suspended above the furniture of the room. Such layouts are usually limited to a maximum depth of about 18in (457mm); this is plenty of space for N gauge track and a reasonable depth of scenery.

If there is no room within the house, consider the loft. This offers a potentially huge space, which would allow for a large N gauge layout with very long trains. Be careful to ensure that correct flooring is installed and do not make any structural alterations to roof supports without consulting a builder. A proper loft conversion would be a good investment, especially with access via stairs or at least a foldaway loft ladder. Otherwise, a loft can be subject to huge temperature variations – from perishing cold in winter to stifling hot in summer. Such temperature ranges can cause track to expand and even buckle.

Moving outside the house, the next room to consider is a garden shed, the most commonly sized being 6ft × 8ft (1,829mm × 2,438mm). This gives a good-sized space for an oval N gauge layout with room for plenty of track and a fair bit of scenery. Things to consider when using a shed for a model railway are: safe but efficient insulation for walls, floor and ceiling; secondary or double-glazing for windows; a safely installed mains electrical supply; a better lock than just a padlock for security and possibly some kind of alarm.

If no room-sized space is available, consider building a layout into a piece of furniture, such as a bookcase. The width of a bookcase is probably limited to about 2ft (610mm) but this allows plenty of room for an N gauge layout. That's even enough depth to fit a full semi-circle of track at just over the minimum recommended radius of 9in (229mm), which will give you an oval layout.

N gauge is one of the few scales that offers the possibility of building an entire layout that will fit onto a dining table. The minimum 9in (229mm) radius means that a double-track loop can be fitted onto a baseboard that's less than 2ft (610mm) wide. When not in use, the layout is easily stored in a cupboard or under a bed.

If none of these potential spaces is on hand, then you need to contemplate building a portable layout. There's actually less of a limitation on space with a portable layout, as long as you've got a large enough space in which to temporarily erect it. The main design considerations for portable layouts are that they need to be lightweight (for moving and storing), easy to set up and break down, strong (to withstand constant handling) and safe to store (such as bolting two baseboards facing each other to protect the layout while in store).

N gauge is flexible enough to be used for a small tabletop layout that can go on the kitchen or dining table and the minimum radius will allow oval layouts to be built, as well as end-to-end types. The baseboards can be smaller to facilitate storage in a cupboard or under the stairs. N gauge not only uses half the length of OO gauge, it is also half the height, which makes it practical to store baseboards under a bed (though remember to cover them to keep the dust off).

STARTING WITH A TRAIN SET

You may fondly remember having a train set when you were young, so it's reasonable to think about buying an N gauge train set as a starting point. There are advantages and disadvantages to buying a train set, so it's worth assessing these and looking at possible alternatives.

For British outline modelling, both Graham Farish by Bachmann and Dapol produce what would be considered a traditional train set. These tend to utilize items from the main range, and when one combination of locomotive and rolling stock has sold out, they are not produced again. Some of the contents of the train sets can be unique liveried and numbered models, so they can sell out quickly to collectors. Therefore, you can be limited to what's on offer at the time. However, if you just want to have a play with some N gauge, everything's in the box that you need to get started.

Every train set comes with an oval of sectional track. This is easy to slot together, with a small radius so that it can soon be set up on a table. Also included will be a DC controller and a track connector to get the power from the controller to the track. You will get a locomotive and either a couple of coaches or a small selection of wagons. This is enough to get a feel for N gauge, how it goes on the track and how the rolling stock couples together. It only takes a matter of minutes to assemble everything out of the box and have an N gauge train running round.

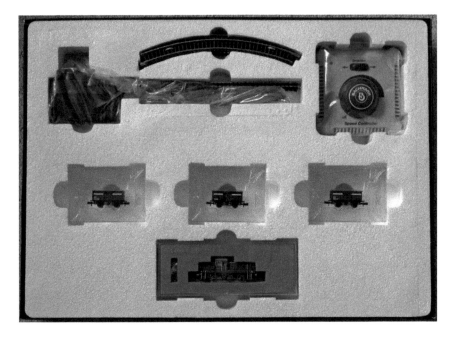

This train set from Graham Farish by Bachmann contains everything that you need to get started: an oval of track; a controller (with a mains power adaptor); a locomotive; some rolling stock. It's a simple and cost-effective way of having a quick experiment with N gauge to see what the scale has to offer.

This is the basic oval of track from the Graham Farish by Bachmann train set, with minimum radius curved track. It's as basic as you can get, and you will soon find it limiting; however, it's hard to deny the initial excitement of seeing the train going round.

Some train sets may include a turnout for a siding, but very quickly you will find that a train set feels limited in what it can do – basically, running round and round. They are phenomenal value for money for what you get, as the included components would cost you much more if you bought them separately. This is great if you just want to try out N gauge, but as you will certainly want to take it further there are a couple of reasons for not buying a train set.

With a train set, you are limited to the rolling stock that's included, which may not be the prototype that you are interested in. You might be better to buy the individual items of rolling stock that you actually want, and you can gradually build up your collection as you go along. Alternatively, look out for train packs, which consist of a locomotive and complementary set of wagons or coaches. These are a sort of train set but without the track and controller.

You can also buy a track pack such as the sectional track one produced by Peco. This is like a train set but without the trains; however, it is more flexible than basic train-set track as there are two turnouts, as well as an oval of track, so you can have a few sidings to do some shunting. Also included is an excellent track plans book with ideas for layouts using the track pack as a starting point. As Peco track is pretty much universal in N gauge, it's easily extended with additional components.

The controller included in a train set will only be a single-track controller. If you are planning to build a double-track layout, you will need to purchase an additional controller. You can buy twin- or even quadruple-track controllers, which may be a more economical choice than buying additional single controllers.

The rolling stock in this Graham Farish by Bachmann train set consists of a Class 14 diesel shunter in National Coal Board (NCB) livery and three matching wagons (each with different numbers printed on them). They are all superb models and great value for money in a train set, but you are limited to the colour and selection on offer.

This is the same Class 14 model as the one in the train set, but it was purchased separately, so that the alternative British Railways green livery could be chosen. The wagons were also purchased separately, so that the different types could be selected. While train sets are good value for money, buying the items individually allows you to pick and choose exactly what you want for the model railway you are setting out to build.

This track pack from Peco is worth considering as an alternative to buying a train set. It comes with more track than you would get in a train set, not least a couple of turnouts. There is also an extremely good track plans book included, to help you get started with ideas for your model railway.

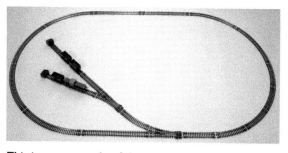

This is one example of the numerous configurations possible with the Peco track pack. There's still an oval to let the trains run round and round but the addition of some turnouts starts to introduce the idea of further operational possibilities. Once the potential of the track pack itself starts to feel limiting, it is a simple matter to extend it further with additional components from the Peco range.

TYPES OF LAYOUT

Model railway layouts come in all shapes and sizes. There is no rule that says how big or small a layout should be. You will see some common types of layout, so it's worth taking a look at these to see what they offer and how that might influence the N gauge layout that you want to build.

OVAL LAYOUTS

If you've made a start by buying a train set or a track pack, then you will already have an oval of track. A train set is always packaged with an oval of track because it's simple to put together and it lets the trains run ad infinitum. Oval layouts are also referred to as 'loop' layouts (because the track loops back on itself) or 'continuous run' layouts (because the trains can run round without any need for interaction from the operator).

On an oval layout, the trains never go anywhere; they just pass through either one or more stations, a rural or urban scenic setting, or a combination of some or all of these. The trains just go round and round. If you just want to sit back and relax by enjoying watching the trains go by, then an oval layout is for you. You might think that this enjoyment could soon wane by watching the same train going past time after time. You can double the entertainment; rather than a single track, a double track allows one train to go clockwise and another to go anticlockwise.

Even this may pall after a while, so what you need is a way to easily change the entire train. This is where a fiddle yard comes in, as it allows a rota of trains to go round the layout. Even a modest-sized fiddle yard can send a large enough sequence of trains around the layout, such that it is some time before it repeats. The generally accepted wisdom is to put a fiddle yard on one straight side of a loop with a station on the other side. Both sides are connected by the semicircles of track at each end.

The station on one side gives you the excuse to stop passenger trains. If the station has a goods yard, you can stop freight trains and do a bit of shunting. So you can watch the trains just roll by or you can interact with the layout at the station. For this reason, oval layouts are always popular as they give you the best of both worlds. There's no need to turn trains round to send them back again, they can just keep going round and round. An oval layout is always ready for action whether you have five minutes or five hours; you can just turn the power on and have trains running round straight away.

In the larger scales, the only practical option for an oval layout is to build it around the walls of a room. The size of the radii required to loop back through a semicircle means that you need quite a bit of space. This also means that you need to sit within the oval, which you can if the layout runs around the extremities of the room. There's nothing to stop you building an N gauge layout around the walls in the same way. This will give you a nice big layout with plenty of space for the layout to breathe. If a room-sized space is not available to you, N gauge is small enough to fit a reasonable oval layout onto a single baseboard. This can be a portable layout that can be operated on a table, or in a standalone capacity on its own supports.

Key ■ Station ▨ Scenic divider ■ Fiddle yard ▨ Scenic area

An oval layout will fit on one baseboard in N gauge or it can be run around an entire room. Whatever the size, the most common design is to have a station on one side and a fiddle yard on the other. You can restrict the scenic area to hide the curves, as in the left-hand diagram, or put a scenic break down the centre of the layout, as with the middle diagram. The right-hand diagram is a double-sided layout with a station on each side, separated by the scenic divider in the middle.

Because you can get a semicircle of N gauge track into a baseboard depth of less than 2ft (610mm) you can build a long, thin, oval layout. This could also be a portable standalone layout, or supported on a shelf along a single wall of a room. This can still take the form of a station at the front with a fiddle yard at the back. Such long layouts allow plenty of room for scenery either side of one or more stations, while the fiddle yard is so long that very long trains are easily accommodated. If shorter trains are modelled, they can be stacked one in front of another on the long fiddle-yard tracks. Many N gauge exhibition layouts take this form as operators can stand at the back with the scenic portion on view to the public at the front. If you do make a layout like this, make sure that you can easily access the fiddle yard at the rear of the layout.

TERMINUS LAYOUTS

Whereas on an oval layout the trains never go anywhere, only through somewhere, if you model a terminus, you definitely get a feeling of arriving. A terminus is the end of the line. As you can't go any further, you can only go back the way you came. There's no way, therefore, that you can just sit and watch the trains go by. A terminus requires locomotives to be run round to the other end of the train. In other words, a terminus is very much about hands-on operation. So if you like to interact with your layout at all times, then the terminus could be for you.

A terminus can be as small as the end of a rural branch line in the middle of nowhere or it can be as big as a huge city station. However big you want it, the functions are the same, just their frequency and complexity are different. Any train that arrives has to be prepared to return from whence it came. For locomotive-hauled trains, this means getting the incoming locomotive onto the other end.

The round and round nature of an oval layout means that you don't actually need to do any shunting if you do not want to. Trains can be permanently coupled into fixed rakes and you never need to touch the stock. This is definitely not an option at a terminus, so you need to consider the ease of coupling and uncoupling in N gauge in order to carry out run-round manoeuvres and shunting.

Unlike the depth required for the radii of an oval layout, a terminus layout can be quite thin and as long as you want. The common approach to a terminus layout is to have a station at one end and a fiddle yard at the other. Bear in mind that unless you can have a considerable distance between the two, the time taken to travel from the fiddle yard to the station may be measured in seconds. This means that trains are not visibly in motion for very long, the opposite of an oval layout; however, the terminus is all about operation, so this should not matter.

Imagine an oval layout with a semicircle at one end only. The oval layout has become a terminus layout but instead of being long and thin, it is now deep and compact. The fiddle yard is behind the station, as with an oval layout, and the semicircle that is left at one end is the transition from one to the other. A long, thin terminus layout connected to a fiddle yard layout needs to be along a wall or on a shelf. By putting the fiddle yard behind the station, you can make a portable N gauge layout that is small enough to fit on top of a table.

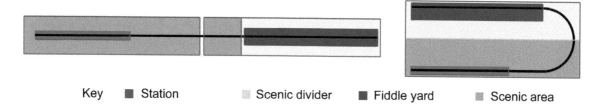

Key   ■ Station   Scenic divider   ■ Fiddle yard   Scenic area

Terminus layouts are just as popular as oval layouts, though you cannot just sit and watch the trains go by. They can be long and thin, as with the diagram on the left, which is ideal for a layout on a shelf or on a bookcase. You can still fit everything on to one tabletop baseboard with N gauge if you need to, by curving it back on itself like an oval layout but with only one curve.

COMBINATION LAYOUTS

Do not think that you have to limit yourself to just having an oval layout or a terminus layout. There is nothing to stop you combining the two as many times as you like. The simplest combination is to add a terminus to an oval and link them together with a junction. The terminus can go inside or outside the loop, or even over part of the loop – a common design is to put a terminus over the fiddle yard to hide it (though remember to leave enough room to access the fiddle yard). You might have room for more than one terminus.

Running a track diagonally from one corner of the loop to the other forms a reverse loop, which permits 'out and back' running from the terminus. A train can leave the terminus, run clockwise around the loop, take the diagonal to reverse its direction, run anticlockwise around the loop and then arrive back at the terminus. This allows you to watch the trains go by as well as have the operational enjoyment of dealing with trains at a terminus. The reverse loop means that you do not have to physically turn the train around to return it to the terminus. You can make this design as big as a room, or small enough in N gauge to fit onto a single baseboard that will sit on a tabletop.

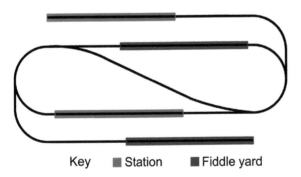

Key ■ Station ■ Fiddle yard

N gauge allows you to get more into less space. If you have the space, consider a layout that is a combination of as many basic layout types as you desire. This design has a terminus, a through station, an oval for continuous running, two fiddle yards and a diagonal track to reverse trains back the way they came. Incredibly, all this action can be made to fit on to one baseboard with N gauge. It can even be made to fit on an average-sized table.

CHOOSING A PROTOTYPE

First and foremost, choosing what prototype you want to model is a purely personal decision. Sensible railway modellers refer to 'rule one', which goes something like this – it's your train set so you can run whatever you want. It all depends where your interests lie; however, that can define the type of layout you need. Alternatively, if available space is an issue, then that can define what you are able to model.

If you want the excitement of very long trains hurtling along a main line, you probably want an oval layout with a station on one side and a fiddle yard full of trains on the other. It needs to be quite long to accommodate those very long trains. While you can pack a lot of N gauge into a small space, the chances are that you will not fit it on to a tabletop and you will need a room-sized space. At the other extreme, if you want the sleepy nature of a country branch line with short passenger and pickup goods trains, you would probably model a terminus layout. Somewhere in between lies a whole plethora of possible layouts that will give you the best of both worlds.

You can slavishly model a real place and that is extremely rewarding; however, modest stations can be huge affairs in real life, so that even in N gauge, you may not have room to fit it all in. Most model railway layouts, therefore, represent a place that is a fiction, although usually with its roots in a plausible reality. You can take the readily available model buildings from a number of real places and use them to build a station that has the character of those real places or the general area. Often it is down to personal taste – you may want more sidings, or possibly an engine shed, which a real place never had. You can mix and match to your heart's content.

Having decided on the type of layout you want, and the type of operation, you can more closely define the era that you wish to model. The 'era system' is a useful, though not totally definitive, guide to the period over which rolling stock was used. It is useful to refer to the following five broad periods in Britain's railway history.

Pre-grouping layouts are rare in N gauge as with most railway modelling, although manufacturers occasionally produce appropriate rolling stock, such as this model by Dapol of a London & South Western Railway M7 0-4-4T; the real locomotive was built in 1897 and is now part of the National Collection.

PRE-GROUPING

This covers anything from the dawn of the railways through their heyday to the beginnings of decline, which resulted in the grouping in 1923. During this period there were hundreds of separate railway companies on a very regional basis. As a result, it's a fascinating time with a multiplicity of locomotives and liveries; however, it's probably the least popular with modellers.

This lack of interest means that it is not well supported by the manufacturers in N gauge. There are a few locomotives available that are suitable, though the much regionalized nature of railways in this period means that these few are spread far and wide and possibly too thinly for most layouts. There are not many suitable coaches, although wagons fare a little better – many goods wagons survived well into the later periods, so they are reasonably well represented in N gauge. Ultimately, to model a pre-grouping railway will probably require a lot of modification and repainting of rolling stock.

GROUPING THROUGH TO NATIONALIZATION

The huge war effort of the many separate railway companies during the First World War left Britain's railway network in a poor state. While nationalization was considered, the eventual solution was rationalization by consolidating the numerous individual railway companies (which were often inefficiently competing

against one another). This was the so-called grouping of 1923, which resulted in the 'big four' of the Great Western Railway, the London Midland and Scottish Railway, the London and North Eastern Railway, and the Southern Railway.

These companies now covered far greater territories than their pre-grouping counterparts, although they continued to use the rolling stock from the amalgamations, as well as building their own. This period is still popular with modellers, with locations often chosen to include trains from two of the four companies. It is also quite well supported by manufacturers, with most of the key locomotive types offered in N gauge. Some accurate coaching stock is available, while the many and varied goods wagons of the period are well represented.

BRITISH RAILWAYS

The Second World War placed even greater demands on the railway infrastructure, leaving it once again exhausted. At the end of 1947 the big four were finally nationalized, the result being British Railways. However, the influence of the big four lasted a long time, and British Railways even continued to build rolling stock to the pre-nationalization designs until it had developed its own standard designs. At the same time, British Railways started its modernization plan, which would ultimately replace steam with diesel. The withdrawal of the last steam locomotives in 1968 marks the end of this period.

The 'grouping' era is well represented by N gauge manufacturers, as most of the rolling stock lasted into the next era (and often preservation). This Great Western Railway scene on Tunley Marsh has all the charm of the inter-war years. Note the typical private-owner coal wagon in the goods train and also the LMS van; the 'big four' regularly exchanged their wagons under common-user agreements, which gives modellers the chance for more variety.

This period of consolidation and then rapid change continues to be the most popular amongst railway modellers, and N gauge is no exception. The variety of rolling stock that could be observed in the transition period ranged from the pre-war steam locomotive designs of the big four to the newly introduced diesels and electrics, with British Railways' own standard steam locomotives in between. Coaches and wagons were equally diverse.

From a modelling point of view, it's no wonder that this period is by far the most popular, not least because it's within living memory for many. It is possibly the best period in terms of support from the manufacturers, including as it does the big four designs from the previous period and modernization designs that would dominate in the next period. These are well represented by the manufacturers, although the British Railways' standard steam loco-motives are only just becoming available. If you want sheer variety in your rolling stock, then you can do no better than this period for the absolute breadth of available models.

BRITISH RAIL

The change from British Railways to British Rail was perhaps just a notional one, as it was still a nationalized entity. While the move to an all-encompassing corporate identity started prior to the abolition of steam in 1968, that year is such a significant milestone that it serves as a useful date to define the start of the next period. The corporate image of the all-encompassing blue and grey livery lasted well over a decade, until British Rail's move to the new sector-orientated organizational model seemed to have the opposite effect – many and various liveries became the order of the day.

By far the most popular era for N gauge modellers is the British Railways period from nationalization to modernization. Part of this popularity is due to being able to run such a broad range of motive power, particularly steam locomotives alongside diesels. This is represented in this scene on Glazebrook by the Warrington Model Railway Club, where a 4F steam locomotive (actually a pre-nationalization LMS design) meets a 'modern' Type 2 diesel (later known as Class 24).

The British Rail era from the end of steam to privatization was, until recently, a little overlooked by modellers, despite always being well supported by manufacturers in N gauge. It's actually a fascinating time, as modernization became standardization before giving way to sectorization. This scene on Growler Street is very much a late 1980s one, even though the locomotives would have been thirty years old by then.

Most of the locomotive fleet originated in the British Railways modernization plan and was still going strong. The relatively small range of locomotive types (compared to the British Railways period) means that fewer models cover a greater percentage of the types. This means that the period is extremely well represented by the manufacturers. Steam-era coaches gave way to later standard types and these are also well represented. Like the locomotive fleet in the British Railways period, the wagon fleet underwent an extensive modernization, although pre-war designs lasted until replaced by modern high-volume, air-braked equivalents. The latter are surprisingly well represented by manufacturers. This means that it's quite easy to model the British Rail period in N gauge, as virtually all the major types of rolling stock and livery are now available.

PRIVATIZATION

British Rail was broken up and privatized from 1994, although the only noticeable difference was the gradual introduction of yet more liveries on to the existing (and sometimes still British Railways-designed) rolling stock. These liveries have continued to change as the owners and franchise operators themselves change. Fortunately, as a lick of paint is often the only difference, the models available from the previous period are suitable.

New locomotive traction has been confined to the Class 66 and Class 70, both of which are available in N gauge. The real railway has largely eliminated locomotive-hauled passenger trains, their replacements being multiple units of varying size. Thankfully, several manufacturers have produced these in N gauge. New

The post-privatization era is the railway you can see today with many colourful and exciting liveries. This scene shows a Stobart Rail liveried Class 66 hauling containers on Mike Le Marie's exhibition layout Garsdale Head. The 'elderly' Class 25 is running on a preserved railway that Mike has included alongside the main line.

wagon types continue to appear, not least for the bulk commodity handling that the modern railway does so well and the ever-expanding need to move containers. Once again, these new prototypes are well represented by the manufacturers in N gauge.

This is very much the current period and its popularity with modellers means that manufacturers of N gauge models will undoubtedly continue to develop new models as the real railway itself develops them. The popularity of this period is that you can go out and see it for real as it is now, unlike any of the previous periods where you are reliant on archive material or preserved railways. This popularity is also apparent amongst younger modellers, who are enthused by being able to model the trains that they are growing up with. Thankfully, manufacturers are supporting the era, as it means that they are helping to encourage the next generation of railway modellers.

DEVELOPING A TRACK PLAN

Having decided where your layout will go, the type of layout and what prototype you want to model, you might be tempted to dive straight in to building your N gauge layout. Take some time to do a little bit of design, so as to avoid mistakes later on. You can develop your model railway as you go along, if that's how you enjoy modelling, but a modicum of design will avoid potential frustrations later on.

Do have a look at other people's track plans in books and magazines for inspiration and ideas. You can copy any plan slavishly or just use the 'best bits' that really interest you. Some of these will be N gauge ones but plans in larger scales are still relevant. The length and depth of an OO gauge layout can be halved to see how big it will be in N gauge.

CURVES

Traditionally, the minimum radius in N gauge was 9in (230mm). Most rolling stock will just about run round this minimum radius; however, some manufacturers, making a modern generation of model locomotives, are publishing a minimum radius closer to 12in (305mm). Even a 12in radius is a lot tighter than a real radius. There is a trade-off between the greater

fidelity of these modern models against the 'train set' appearance of very tight curves. Just like real trains, your model trains will generate greater friction on the track as they pass into the curves. Modern locomotive models are very powerful, and the rolling stock is very freewheeling, but it is something to be aware of. Don't attempt a platform on a tight corner, as the gap between the platform and coaches will be unrealistic. If a tight corner is workable but simply not pleasing to the eye, consider hiding it within a tunnel or cutting.

The gap between two railway lines is referred to as 'the four foot'. The middle section of a bogie coach on the outer line of the curve will overhang the four foot while the front of a large steam loco on the inner line will hang into the four foot. The result is the potential for a collision, more so in N gauge where the smaller scale means that clearances may be tighter. Proprietary N gauge track systems tend to increase width of the four foot slightly to make sure that there is a generous gap between the tracks to avoid collision.

TURNOUTS

Real railways build their turnouts precisely to fit a specific location. Thankfully, the model track manufacturers in N gauge produce a range of turnouts, which are integrated into the geometry of curved sectional track.

Every turnout has at least one curve to it in order to diverge the track away in a different direction. Just like the sectional track, you can get some turnouts with a pretty tight radius. The greater the radius of a turnout, the more realistic it will be. This is less obvious in goods yards when you are shunting at a slow speed. However, consider an express train changing from the fast line to the slow line at speed – using sectional track and tight radius turnouts, the train will wiggle one way then the other and might even derail. The larger radius of so-called 'express turnouts' will make the train snake smoothly from one track to the other.

FROM THE BACK OF AN ENVELOPE

Start with rough sketches before you do any detailed planning. This allows you to try out your ideas and the

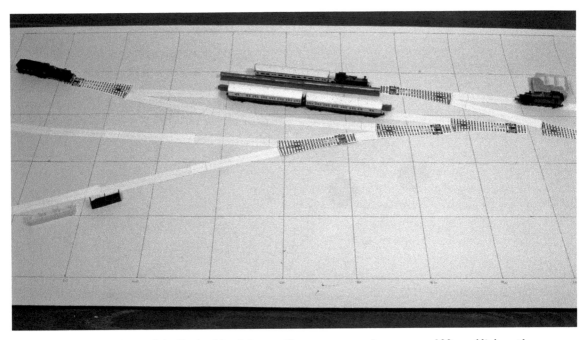

This is a full-size mock-up of the Tunley Marsh layout. The squares are drawn every 100mm (4in) on the back of a piece of wallpaper. The turnouts are paper templates from Peco, which exactly match their turnout range, while the 'track' is just strips of paper. A few structures and some items of rolling stock help to give a feel for how the finished layout will look.

inspirations. It's easy enough to discard these 'back of an envelope' drawings if they are not what you like. When you've settled on the ideas that you want, do another sketch and imagine what the plan will be like to operate. This way, you can determine whether there is enough operational potential to sustain your interest when the layout is built.

It's useful to have a few key measurements. For example, you need to know how long your coaches are if you are going to make a run-round loop that is long enough to hold them. Similarly, you may want to check that sidings will be long enough to hold the number of wagons that you want.

Armed with your sketched plan and key measurements, you can draw the proposed plan a little more formally. You need nothing more than some graph paper, a pencil, a compass and a ruler; the squares on the graph paper will allow you to draw even quite a large plan at a reduced scale. If the layout will be a more modest affair, N gauge is small enough that you can probably draw the plan full size. The back of

a piece of wallpaper is a cheap and ready supply of paper on which to do this. It's useful to draw some squares on to the paper as reference points.

If you are drawing the plan to full size, you can use a few pieces of actual track and some turnouts, either to see how the plan will look or as templates around which to draw. If you don't want to buy any track at this stage, Peco produce paper templates for their entire N gauge turnout range; you can copy these as many times as you want and just use a ruler to draw in the plain track in between.

If you're feeling a bit more high-tech than pen and paper, there are a number of cheap and easily mastered Computer Aided Design (CAD) programs available, which allow you to draw everything 'virtually' and print off the end result. Perhaps a better option is one of the increasing ranges of bespoke track-planning programs. These often have all the main track manufacturers' N gauge components included and will work out any tricky bits of track geometry for you.

FIDDLE YARDS

You don't have to have a fiddle yard on an N gauge model railway, but without one you may find that your layout becomes inflexible. While you may be happy just to watch a couple of trains going round now, it's a sure thing that you will want to buy more trains in the future. These won't all fit on the layout at the same time, so you a need way to swap them round. You can do this by hand on the layout if you want, but a safer, quicker and more flexible solution is to use a fiddle yard.

A fiddle yard counters one of the things that can put some modellers off N gauge, namely the small size of the rolling stock and potential difficulties of getting it on the track. If you only have to do this once, and can leave it in the fiddle yard to run on the layout whenever you want, then you need not worry about handling the smaller-size models.

The rest of the railway world is represented by the fiddle yard. It is the rest of the railway network that the stations on your layout are connected to. Fiddle yards are sometimes called 'staging' (an American term), 'storage tracks' or 'hidden sidings'; each term is suitably descriptive. Although there are many different types of fiddle yard, they all perform the same function of being the rest of the world.

A fiddle yard can be as simple as a single piece of track, literally one siding off the layout; however, this requires a lot of handling of stock every time you want to swap to another train. A ladder fiddle yard has as many sidings as you need, though they only need to be as long as the longest train that you will run. This type of fiddle yard can be used for a terminus to fiddle yard layout or, by joining all the sidings to the main line at the other end, it can be used on an oval layout.

A sector plate has a base (the plate) that is pivoted at one end, so that a series of curved sidings on it (the sector) can be aligned with the main line. It is only suitable for terminus to fiddle yard type layouts. For oval layouts, or just the ability to turn an entire train without handling, you can use a turntable. This describes a full circle, which can take up a lot of room; however, the smaller size of N gauge makes a turntable a practical proposition.

A traverser is simply a piece of baseboard with parallel sidings that slides at a right angle to the main line. You can mount it onto drawer runners or simply

The fiddle yard used on Tunley Marsh is a traverser. Seven trains can be stored and each one accesses the layout by simply aligning the traverser with the track that goes through the back scene. The traverser can be removed from the supporting baseboard so that it can be turned through 180 degrees and then placed back. This allows the trains arriving from the layout to be turned around without the need to handle the rolling stock. Note the 'buffers' made from pieces of dowel at the end of each track to prevent trains accidentally falling off.

slide it on batons or use the kind of slippery surfaces found on some hardboard materials, such as laminate flooring.

Cassettes are like trays or boxes into which you can drive a train and then pick it up without having to actually touch the model. They usually have a single track because the walls of the cassette protect the rolling stock and prevent it tipping over when it is moved. Cassettes are quite easy to make and provide a brilliant solution for N gauge as it's possible to lift and turn all but the longest of trains in this smaller scale.

Always consider a fiddle yard for your layout, especially in N gauge. Your rolling-stock collection will soon outgrow your layout without one. Fiddle-yard solutions mean that you can store more trains on your layout, so you won't have to keep putting them in and out of boxes and re-railing them as you put them on the layout. By not having a fiddle yard, you could be handling your rolling stock a lot. Any kind of handling can inadvertently lead to damage to the fine detail on today's superb models. Worst of all, it's so easy to drop models, no matter how careful you are.

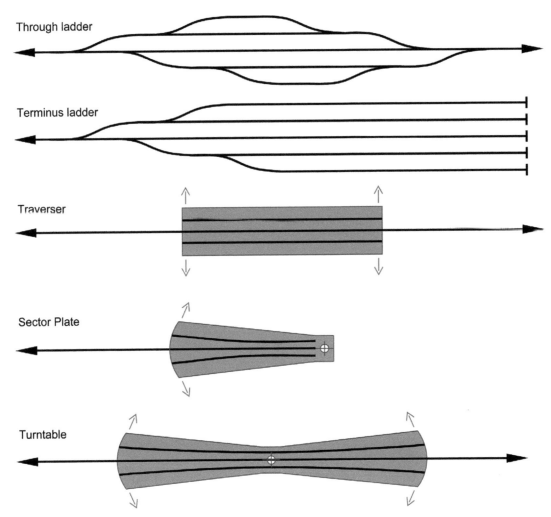

There are many types of fiddle yard, each being best for a different situation. The 'ladder types' (through or terminus) are easy to build, as they just require track to be laid. The mechanical fiddle yards (traverser, sector plate and turntable) require a little more skill to build them into a baseboard, to make them move and to align the tracks; however, their flexibility and compactness make them ideal fiddle-yard solutions.

CHAPTER THREE

BASEBOARDS

The baseboards are literally the foundation on which your N gauge layout will be built. Just like building a house, if you get this stage right, you won't have any problems developing the rest of the layout. They need to be strong enough so that the layout will not sustain any damage, especially if it is a portable layout that is being frequently moved. Yet if they are portable, they need to be light enough for easy movement. You also need to consider what goes under a baseboard, such as wiring and turnout motors. Most of the aspects of baseboard construction in N gauge are no different to any other scale.

Even a permanent layout should be portable to some extent, because you might need to move it. Even without something as disruptive as a house move, you might need to move the layout out of a room for decorating or home maintenance. It's also beneficial for a number of tasks, as you are building the layout. You may want to spray the track with an aerosol paint, which is a less malodorous experience if you can take the baseboard outside. Even for inside tasks, such as wiring, it is a lot easier to be able to put the baseboard on its side rather than having to crawl around underneath it.

If your layout will be moved on a regular basis, the weight of individual baseboards is vitally important. Wood comes in varying types and qualities. Some is best avoided, such as chipboard, which is very heavy as well as being hard to cut. There are plenty of good reasons for keeping your baseboards light but strong. You will feel less inclined to reach out and enjoy the operation of your finished layout if it is heavy and cumbersome to move.

TRADITIONAL BASEBOARD FRAMES

When you choose how to build your baseboard, the two considerations are: what you will make the frame out of, and what you will make the top out of. There has always been a traditional way to make baseboards, using a wooden frame. In the last few decades, some modellers have experimented with different constructional methods, principally to reduce weight while maintaining or increasing strength.

Despite the increasing use of alternative materials in everyday life, wood remains the baseboard material of choice for railway modellers. It's easy to see why, as it is straightforward to work with, reasonably inexpensive and very flexible. If you don't trust your woodworking skills, there's always the option of employing a professional carpenter. There are several firms that do nothing else but make baseboards for model railways, and these will all be suitable for N gauge.

The so-called 'traditional' baseboard frame has been made for many years out of 2in by 1in (50mm by 25mm) timber. Note that 'planed all round' timber is actually smaller than the notional measurements quoted. Wood is easy to cut, then glue and screw together to make a frame, with cross-members to support the top. It's quite adequate for a baseboard of about 4ft (1,219mm) long by 2ft (610mm) wide. To make the baseboard larger, it may be better to use the next size up of timber.

If you are using equipment under the baseboard, such as motors for signals, you may need a deeper baseboard frame anyway to accommodate these larger objects. Unfortunately, this makes things heavier by using bigger pieces of wood. For modest-sized permanent or portable N gauge layout baseboards, the 'two by one inch' framed baseboard is still just as good today as it ever was.

If you are reasonably comfortable with basic woodworking skills, then building a simple traditional framed baseboard will be well within your capabilities. You only require a few simple tools, such as a

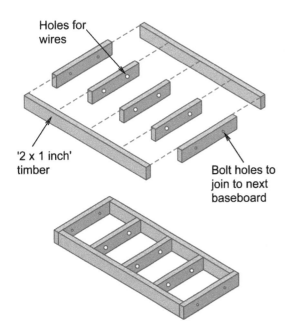

Holes for wires

'2 x 1 inch' timber

Bolt holes to join to next baseboard

A traditional baseboard frame is easily constructed from wood, with planed 'two by one' inch timber as a minimum. Do check that pieces of timber are as straight as possible, as softwood has a tendency to warp; buying from a timber merchant is often the better option, as individual pieces can be checked, unlike the pre-packed timber bundles in DIY stores. Remember to cut some holes in the cross-braces for running wires under the layout.

tenon saw, hammer, drill, screwdriver, clamps, ruler and square, although you can invest in power tools, such as a compound mitre saw, for larger projects or regular layout building.

First of all, you need some wood. Varying lengths of softwood timber are quite cheap, so you can afford to make the odd mistake. Wood is, of course, organic, so no two pieces are the same, and it can warp or twist. A slight deviation from true can be corrected once all the parts of the frame are joined, as screws can pull everything back into square. You can buy timber from DIY stores or timber merchants. DIY stores tend to bulk-package lengths of timber and although this is cheaper, you cannot check each piece to see if it is straight. At timber merchants, everything tends to be loose, so you can have a good root around to find the best pieces.

Once you have got the timber home, work out what individual pieces you need and prepare a cutting list to avoid wastage. For example, using 6ft (1,830mm) lengths of timber to build a 4ft × 2ft (1,219mm × 610mm) frame with cross-bracing every 1ft (305mm), requires only three pieces of timber: two 4ft (1,219mm) pieces and five 2ft (610mm) pieces.

After cutting the timber, you will have a stack of parts to make a frame. Before assembly, drill holes in the ends of the end pieces and countersink the holes – it is best to use countersink screws (the norm for woodwork) as they will not protrude from the baseboard edge.

The basic sides and ends can now be screwed together. Some people 'screw and glue' but for a traditional frame, wood screws alone are sufficient. Clamp the two pieces that are to be joined to a flat surface and then use a square to check that the corners are at 90 degrees. Using the holes in the end piece, drill pilot holes into the ends of the side pieces, as this makes it easier to add the screws and prevents the wood from splitting. Then screw the two pieces together; crosshead screws and a corresponding bit in a power driver (or electric drill) will speed things up.

Once the sides and ends are together, you have a basic frame, but it will lack strength until the cross-braces are added. Before adding the cross-braces, drill access holes for the eventual installation of the layout wiring, as it will be a lot harder to add these holes once the baseboard is completed. There's no need to add lots of holes or to make them too big, as you may compromise the integrity of the cross-braces.

Adding the cross-braces is a repeat of the process to join the sides and ends. Clamp the frame and cross-brace to a work surface, and use a square to check that they are at 90 degrees to each other. It's easier to drill the pilot holes through the sides and into the ends of the cross-braces at this point, rather than trying to measure where they should be.

These are the only tools you need to cut timber for a baseboard frame, laid out on a Black & Decker Workmate, which is being used to hold a piece of timber. Make sure you 'measure twice and cut once'. The square on the left has been used to draw a line around the piece of timber – this line acts as a guide when sawing, which ensures that you get accurately angled corners and ends.

If you are building a large layout with a lot of baseboards, or build lots of layouts, then the modest expense of a compound mitre saw is a good investment. Compared to hand-sawing, it's much quicker, less effort and you are guaranteed to get perfect square cuts every time. Always follow the safety instructions, be aware of where your fingers are and wear a dust mask, goggles and ear-defenders.

Drill holes at the ends of the end pieces before starting assembly. Use a scrap piece of timber on its side as a guide to draw a pencil line at each end, so that you know where the middle of the edge of the joining piece of timber will be. The top piece shows the holes after being drilled, while the lower piece has the holes countersunk ready for screws.

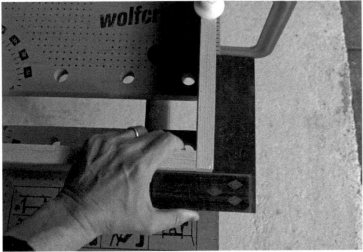

Before joining two pieces to make a corner, clamp them to a flat surface and use a square to ensure that they are at ninety degrees.

Make sure that the screws are driven in all the way so that their heads are flush with the timber. This stops them catching or snagging anything but is particularly important, as here, on the ends, where the frame will be joined to another baseboard.

Before adding the cross-braces, drill access holes for the layout wiring. These cross-braces are 18in (457mm) wide. Start with a pilot hole (seen on the left of both pieces) and then use the spade bit (13mm in this case) to go half-way through (seen on the top piece) before turning over and drilling through from the other side (seen on the lower piece). This stops the spade bit from splintering the wood as it exits the other side.

The cross-braces are added in the same manner as joining the sides and ends, by clamping to a level work surface, drilling pilot holes (which are countersunk), checking with a square and then adding screws.

The addition of the four cross-braces completes the construction of the baseboard frame. The use of a wide-angle lens and the angle from which the photograph was taken make it look as though the sides are bowed outwards, but they are perfectly straight and parallel, held in formation by the cross-braces.

BASEBOARD SURFACES

A baseboard frame needs a top, unless you are building an open-topped frame for the maximum rural scenic potential that is possible with N gauge. A widely used material is ⅜in (9mm) Sundeala. Its advantages are that it is quite soft to cut, and the softness also means that it takes track pins very easily. Despite not being too heavy, without the correct number of cross-members for support, it can be prone to sagging.

Medium Density Fibreboard (MDF) has revolutionized the building trade and furniture design, so it's no surprise to also find modellers using it. Although available in a range of thicknesses, MDF of ⁵⁄₁₆in (8mm) thickness is quite adequate. Tapping in track pins is a bit trickier, since it is a much harder material than Sundeala. It is also much heavier and can double the weight of a baseboard frame. Using MDF for anything larger than a 3ft × 1ft (914mm × 305mm) portable baseboard could make it prohibitively heavy.

Plywood as thin as ⁵⁄₃₂in (4mm) is ideal for a baseboard top. The entire baseboard's strength should be in the frame, so the top is just a covering to put the railway on to. N gauge models are much lighter than ones in the larger scales, so a thin plywood surface is more than adequate.

OPEN-TOPPED BASEBOARDS

An open-topped (or open-frame) baseboard is basically a baseboard without an overall surface material, such as a single piece of MDF. Its main use is for layouts where scenery will be the prime feature. A traditional baseboard with a flat surface does not really represent genuine topography, since very few places in Britain are totally flat. These traditional flat baseboards have tended to have the scenery built up from the datum level of the baseboard surface. This is fine if you are modelling the bottom of a valley; however, what do you do if you want to bridge a river or model a soaring viaduct?

Railway modellers tend to lay the track and then add the scenery. Yet in the real world, the scenery was there first and engineers pushed the railway through the scenery. An open-topped baseboard allows you to design the topography and the railway as a complementary whole. As N gauge offers the chance for stunning scenic vistas, such an approach is worth considering to get the most benefit out of using N gauge for a scenic layout.

The construction of the baseboard's frame is virtually identical to that for a traditional frame baseboard. Obviously, there is no all-encompassing flat top, so what keeps the track up? The answer is a series of

The baseboard frame has now been topped with 4mm plywood. Parallel lines are drawn on the top to correspond to the cross-braces underneath. You could screw the top on to the frame but with thin plywood it is easier to glue and pin it. A good-quality woodworking glue was spread on to the top of the frame before the plywood sheet was added. The pins are small panel pins hammered in every inch or so, and then hammered flush with the surface using a pin punch.

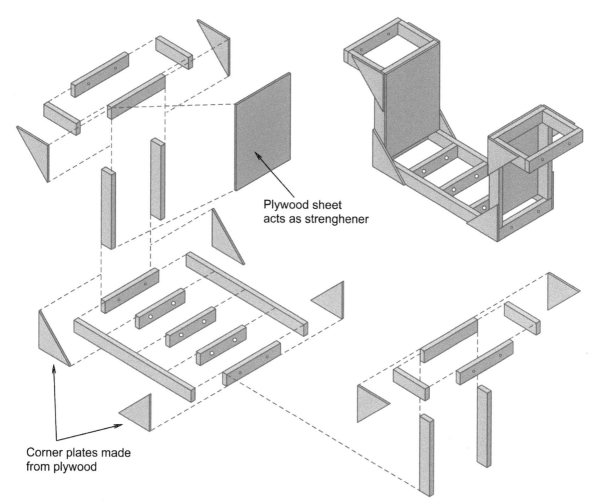

Plywood sheet
acts as strenghener

Corner plates made
from plywood

Railway bridges and viaducts make impressive scenic features but it is necessary to drop the level of the baseboard down as far as the 'bottom of the valley'. It is best to make a separate baseboard frame for this feature, which is at the normal level at either end, but drops to a lower level in the middle. This lower middle portion effectively hangs down from the smaller baseboard sections at each end, the latter being supported by legs and bolted to adjacent baseboards.

formers that will support both the track bed and the contours of the landscape. These formers can be made from thin plywood, as can the track bed, since there is no need for a thick and heavy material, such as MDF, to support the track. The datum level of the frame now acts as the lowest point of the landscape, which rises up to the required height. The railway sits somewhere between the datum level and the highest point, so that it appears to travel through the landscape rather than simply on top of it.

ADDING A BACK SCENE

Most model railway layouts are only viewed from one side, so it is usual to add a back scene to the non-viewing side. Without a back scene, you can see beyond the model world into the real world, which rather distorts the illusion. A permanent room-based layout may not need a back scene, if you are prepared to paint the walls sky blue or even to paint a back scene on to the wall. In most cases, and certainly with portable layouts, you will require a back scene.

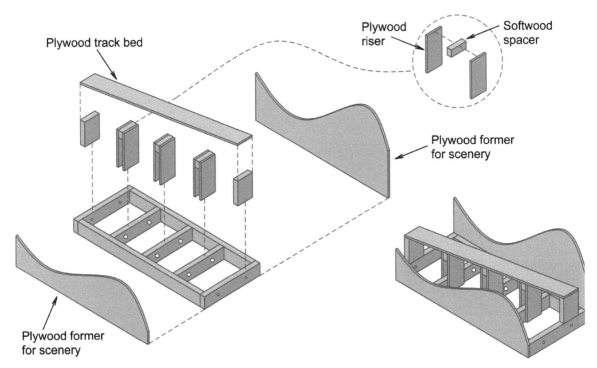

Plywood track bed

Plywood riser

Softwood spacer

Plywood former for scenery

Plywood former for scenery

ABOVE: **Open-top baseboards use a baseboard frame as normal, but there is no single top surface, such as a piece of MDF. The track is supported above the frame on wooden risers. Plywood formers at the front and rear define the basic contours of the scenery, which are filled in between them and the raised track to form the landscape. This is also another method of incorporating bridges and viaducts into the scenery. It is not limited to rural scenery, since this method can be used to elevate a railway 'above the arches' in an urban setting.**

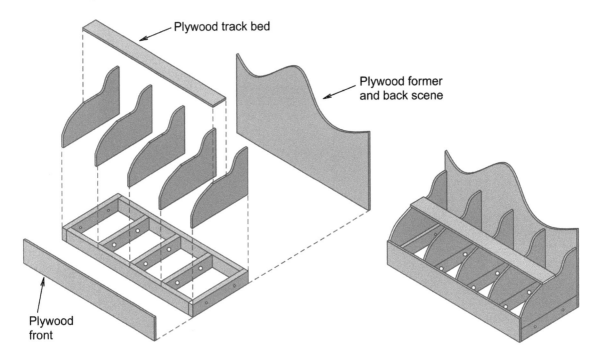

Plywood track bed

Plywood former and back scene

Plywood front

Fortunately, a back scene is very easy to add to a layout. It needs to be no more than a sheet of material that will form the backdrop. Plywood is ideal, though the larger and thinner the piece, the more prone it may be to warping so that it loses its flat shape. Thin MDF remains flatter though it is much heavier. You can buy 'curvy' MDF, which has grooves one side to make it easy to bend into curves. This is ideal for avoiding the abruptness of right-angled corners. Hardboard is thin, durable and perfectly smooth on one side, which is ideal for painting, though larger sheets can be a little heavy. Foam board is smooth-sided and very lightweight, though it may be prone to damage, especially on portable layouts.

Any sheets of wood-based material for a back scene can simply be screwed to the rear of the baseboard frame. It is best to screw it on rather than glue it or nail it on, as it gives you the option to remove it later, if necessary. Make the back scene at the same time as building the baseboards, then remove it for good all-round access while completing the trackwork, then refit it prior to completing the scenery.

RIGHT: *Adding a back scene is a simple case of screwing a sheet of material to the rear of the baseboard frame; in this case, the same 4mm plywood as was used for the baseboard top. It has been aligned with the frame using clamps, before being screwed on. Using screws means that the back scene can be removed while the track is laid, then refitted later.*

BELOW RIGHT: *For end baseboards or single baseboards, it is necessary to add the back scene to the sides of the layout as well. On Tunley Marsh, this is the end that will join to the fiddle yard (which needs to be hidden from view). The plywood for the back scene cannot be screwed to the edge of the baseboard, since this end joins to another baseboard (for the fiddle yard). Therefore, wooden blocks are screwed to the top of the baseboard to support the back scene (these will be hidden later by the scenery). There is a gap between the wooden blocks and a hole in the back scene for the track to run into the fiddle yard.*

OPPOSITE BELOW: *An alternative method of making an open-topped baseboard is to use plywood formers between the rear back scene and the front. These serve the dual purpose of supporting the track bed and forming basic contours for the scenery. The plywood pieces can be glued and pinned to one another but it is worth reinforcing the joints with pieces of wood in the corners (these will be hidden under the scenery).*

PAINTING THE BASEBOARDS

It is not a necessity to paint the visible areas of the baseboards and back scenes. If you are happy with a wood finish, then that's your choice. There are, though, a number of good reasons for painting everything that's beyond the scenic area of the layout, from the aesthetic to the nature of wood itself.

Painting the visible portions of the baseboard frames will give the completed layout a more professional and tidy appearance. It adds nothing from a practical point of view, but it looks nice. Certainly, if you were going to exhibit your layout, you would be expected to paint it as part of a neat and tidy presentation. Colour is a personal choice, though you should avoid any colour that detracts from the actual scenic area of the layout itself. Darker neutral colours, such as black, brown and grey, are best as they persuade the eye to ignore what is beyond the limits of the scenery and concentrate on the layout and not its surroundings.

Wood is an organic product, even man-made versions such as MDF. It interacts with its environment such that changes in temperature, humidity and moisture can cause it to swell or contract. If your layout will be stored or located in an area with potential for extreme changes in these factors, such as a shed or loft, it is worth painting the wood to seal it. You may never totally eliminate the effects of the environment but you can certainly minimize them. For the best protection, paint all the faces of every piece of timber before constructing the baseboard frame. Any covering will do such as primer, varnish, even a thick coat of woodworking glue, as long as it seals the wood against moisture.

SUPPORTING THE LAYOUT

While the baseboards are the foundation for your layout, you still need something to support them, as they won't levitate by themselves. The methods for supporting baseboards tend to relate to the size of the layout and whether it is permanent or portable.

N gauge offers the possibility of building portable layouts that are so small, yet still operationally interesting, that they can be supported by existing house-

hold items. The most obvious of these household items is the kitchen or dining table. The minimum radius in N gauge of 9in (229mm) means that an oval track plan will easily fit onto a tabletop, even allowing a little extra at the sides for some scenery. A table is already set at a comfortable height and comes with chairs that support that comfortable height. Do cover a table with a tablecloth or mats before you put a baseboard on top; even if the baseboard has rubber feet at the corners, the last thing that you want to do is scratch the dining table.

A less obvious household item that can support a baseboard is an ironing board. An ironing board is a design classic – it is height-adjustable and it stores flat when not in use. Once again, N gauge is small enough to make an interesting end-to-end layout that will fit in a maximum space of about 4ft × 1ft (1,219mm × 305mm). This is easily supported by an ironing board; therefore, it is worth considering for small portable N gauge layouts.

Larger portable baseboards (and also permanent ones) can be supported by more traditional means. Folding A-frame trestles provide a firm support for even the largest of baseboards. You can make these from wood, or buy the inexpensive plastic 'saw horse' type sold in DIY stores; they do, however, require quite a bit of storage. A neater solution is fit the baseboard with legs that fold up under and inside the baseboard when not in use.

Finally, if your N gauge layout is quite big and will occupy a room or shed, permanent 'table legs' attached to the baseboard are the simplest and sturdiest solution. However, don't be tempted to build the legs into the baseboard in such a way that the whole layout cannot be easily disassembled in case you ever decide to move house.

JOINING BASEBOARDS

One of the huge advantages of N gauge is that you can build an entire layout that will fit on just one baseboard. This means that you do not have to worry about joining baseboards together every time you want to use a portable layout. If you really want to exploit the potential of N gauge by building a

Trestles such as these sturdy plastic 'saw horse' ones used for Tunley Marsh are a simple way to support a layout. They are ideal for portable layouts since they fold up for storage, but they can also be used where the layout has a permanent location. Note how the smaller fiddle yard board on the right is bolted to the main layout at one end and supported by a removable A-frame leg at the other.

bigger layout, then you will need to join a number of baseboards together. It's not advisable to build one massive room-filling baseboard in case you ever need to take it out of the room to move house. Even a layout that fits onto one baseboard may benefit from having a separate, possibly smaller baseboard, for a fiddle yard.

It's easier than you think to join baseboards — you just have to cater for two things: alignment and

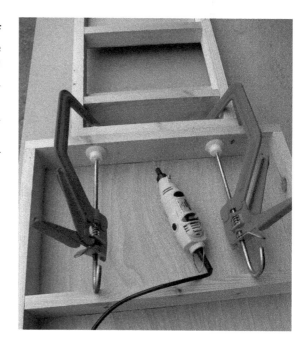

The first and most critical step when joining baseboards is to accurately clamp them together so that they are perfectly aligned, then drill small pilot holes through the ends of both baseboards. The main baseboard (lower) on Tunley Marsh joins to a narrower fiddle-yard baseboard (upper). A mains-powered DIY drill will not fit between the cross-braces, so a smaller hobby drill is used instead to make the pilot holes.

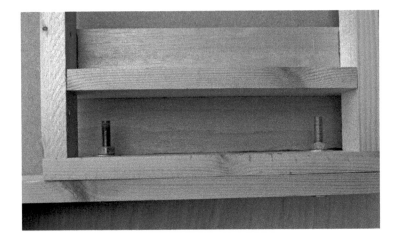

If you are building a permanent layout in a room, it is sufficient to simply bolt the baseboards together, once they have been aligned and clamped. Note the use of a washer behind the nut to avoid damaging the wooden frame.

As the two baseboards on Tunley Marsh are separated for transport and storage, pattern makers' dowels are used for alignment. These consist of two metal plates, one with a point and one with a hole to receive the point. They can be a little tricky to instal but they will ensure perfect alignment every time. For this layout, nuts and bolts are used to keep the baseboards together but there are alternatives, such as suitcase latches.

securing. Of the two, alignment is the most critical. You need the baseboards to join in exactly the same way each time so that the tracks that cross the baseboard joint will line up each time. Even a variance of a millimetre can cause trains to derail at the joint.

There are some commercially available baseboard alignment kits, while a favourite for many years with modellers has been to use pattern-makers' dowels. The first step is to build your baseboard frames and then temporarily clamp them together. It's worth taking the time to make sure that the baseboards are perfectly level with each other. Then drill small pilot holes through the baseboard ends where the alignments will go. The baseboards can now be separated and larger holes drilled in each end, as required, to fit the alignments.

Once the baseboards are brought back together with the installed alignments, they should align perfectly each time. The alignments will not hold the baseboards together. You can use clamps but these can be bulky and untidy. It is better to drill some more holes and bolt the baseboards together. Use washers on the nut side to avoid damaging the wooden baseboard ends. Wing nuts are much quicker to get on and off, while a small electric screwdriver will also speed things up, where the layout needs to be assembled and disassembled regularly. A popular alternative is to use 'suitcase latches' on the side of the baseboard. These are extremely quick to attach and release, and remove the need to fiddle under the baseboard with nuts and bolts. Do look for the more expensive ones, as these usually have a degree of adjustment built in to them.

CHAPTER FOUR

TRACK LAYING

Trains need track on which to run, so once you've constructed your baseboards, it's time to turn the track-plan design of your N gauge layout into a reality. Despite the inevitable excitement that this stage warrants, it needs to be done carefully and methodically. If you do not do a good job laying the track, you may leave yourself open to all sorts of problems in the future. Derailments will be the likely result and that's going to remove all the fun from operating your finished layout. Fortunately, it's not difficult to lay perfect track that will give a lifetime of trouble-free running.

TRACK SYSTEMS IN N GAUGE

Fortunately for N gauge railway modellers, there are a number of track systems, with varying degrees of ease with which they can be used. There are actually slightly more options in N gauge compared with the other commercial scales. Track is track in the sense that each system has two rails to 9mm gauge on which you can run your trains. As you would expect, each track system has its advantages and disadvantages, mainly ease of use versus fidelity to the prototype.

DECIPHERING THE CODE OF THE RAIL

Before looking at a number of track systems, it is helpful to understand a small piece of terminology, namely, the code of the rail (or track). You will see track systems referred to as being 'Code 55' or 'Code 80'. This is not a manufacturer's product code, but actually a measurement. The number in the code is a measure of the height of the rail, measured in one-thousandths of an inch. Therefore, Code 80 track uses rail that is eighty-thousandths of an inch high (0.08in or 2.03mm).

Early track systems tended towards a higher rail, such as Code 80, for two reasons. First, the metal rail in model track gives strength and rigidity to what would otherwise be a very floppy plastic base of sleepers. A piece of track is very hard to bend up or down until you remove the rails, whereupon it will sag under its own weight. The higher the rail, the more strength it gives to the track. This is not really an issue when it's pinned down to a baseboard, it is more to do with handling and packaging the track prior to that.

N gauge modellers are well served by a variety of track systems. This photo shows (left to right): Kato Unitrack; Peco Code 80 sectional track; Peco Code 80 flexible track; Peco Code 55 flexible track; 2mm Scale Association Easitrack.

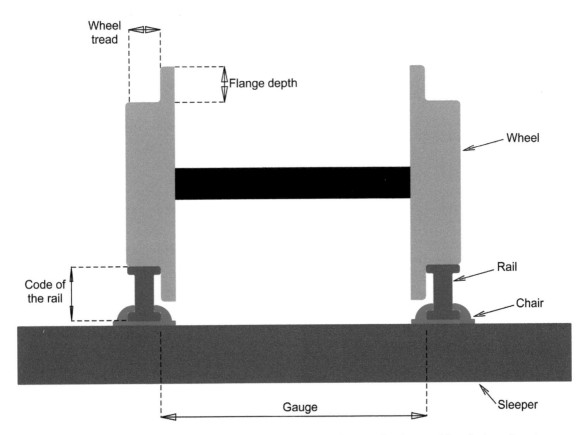

This diagram is not to scale but it illustrates the key dimensions that need to be considered when choosing the 'code' (height) of the rail that you will use in N gauge. Reducing the height of the rail would eventually bring the flange of the wheel into contact with the chairs on the sleepers; however, by using more modern wheels with finer flanges, this will not be a problem.

The second reason for higher rails was actually nothing to do with track at all, rather it was dictated by the rolling stock. Early models had wheels with very deep flanges (the thinner outer part of a wheel that sits inside the rail). Therefore, the rail needed to be high enough to accept the depth of the flange. Otherwise, the flange rides on the chair on the sleeper and lifts the wheel away from the top of the rail, resulting in loss of electrical contact or even derailment. As manufacturing processes have improved, wheel flanges have become finer, such that the height of the rail can be reduced, thus the widespread introduction of Code 55 track for N gauge.

KATO UNITRACK

The Japanese company Kato has been supplying its Unitrack system for several years. It continues to expand, with new components being introduced, and it has become increasingly popular with British modellers. The reason for this popularity can be traced back to its country of manufacture. In Japan, living space is often at a premium, with few opportunities for large, permanent layouts. This explains the dominance of N gauge in Japan and the technical requirements of the Kato track system, whereby many layouts have to be disassembled and packed away at the end of an operating session. This means that the Kato track components have to easily and securely connect to each other, as well as being sufficiently robust to withstand regular handling.

Unitrack is entirely a sectional track system; however, with such a broad range of components, it is

Kato Unitrack is made in Japan, yet it is becoming increasingly popular with British N gauge modellers. Each piece comes with the ballast moulded around the sleepers. It is only just possible to see the join, as here with two straight pieces. If you want a wide range of ready-ballasted track components, it is a system well worth looking at; although, as it is imported, availability can sometimes be an issue.

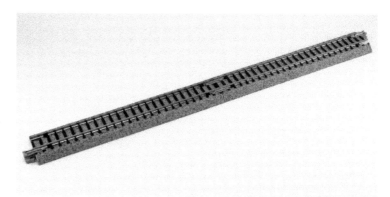

Pieces of Kato Unitrack join together with a satisfyingly firm click but this does not mean that they are impossible to separate. It is a system that is designed to be built and then disassembled at the end of the day. To split the pieces, simply lever them one way until the joiners pop away from each other.

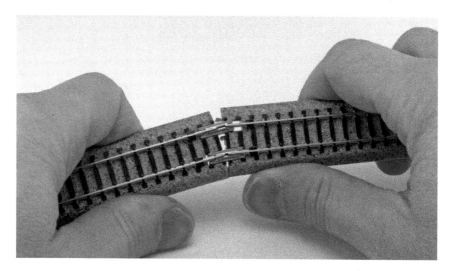

almost as flexible as flexible track. There are four set radii, the smallest being a mere 8in (203mm). While intended to be dismantled and reused, it can be permanently fixed to a layout using pins or glue.

Two features of Unitrack make it stand out for serious consideration. First, the turnout motors are built into the turnouts themselves. This means that there is no need to purchase and fit turnout motors as additional components. They can still be switched manually, if necessary, in which case there is no need to wire power to the turnout motors. However, the turnouts themselves are of the insulated frog type, which may lead to stalling of short-wheelbase locomotives.

The second standout feature of Unitrack is that the track is ready ballasted, in that the rails are attached to a moulded plastic base, which represents both the sleepers and the ballast. Such moulded ballast is not to everyone's taste, and in its raw form, it can just look like plastic rather than stone. As with most plastic finishes, a coat of paint can work wonders. Using one of the so-called 'track and sleeper grime' colours (which tend towards shades of brown) will tone down the grey plastic finish. On permanent layouts, the gaps between parallel tracks can be filled in with a loose ballast; if the painting is done after this stage, both the plastic and loose ballasts can be finished uniformly such that it is hard to see the join.

PECO TRACK

The track system produced by Peco probably accounts for the great majority of track in use on British N gauge layouts. It was first introduced in the 1960s and was probably one of the key foundations responsible for making N gauge a viable modelling scale at that time. Today, the range is extensive, with

As the name suggests, sectional track systems consist of a set of pre-set sections of track that are sufficiently varied as to be able to build an almost limitless number of track plans. These pieces are made by Peco. The straights and curves both include single and double lengths. The turnout is the same length as a single straight, while it's diverging radius is the same as the single-length curve.

both sectional and flexible track, insulated and electrified frog turnouts, complex pieces, such as double slips, and ranges using Code 80 and Code 55 rail. The sheer variety and compatibility of the components undoubtedly makes it the first choice for the N gauge railway modeller.

Starting with the Code 80 sectional track, this offers four complementary radii, the inner being 9in (229mm) and the outermost 13³/₂₅in (333mm). There is a left-hand or right-hand turnout, and three lengths of straight track, even a crossover. Turnouts are the insulated frog type and quite sharp, being the same radius as the inner radius curved track. It's easily joined and pinned down, so it's ideal if you are a beginner with track laying. There is even a range of complementary foam ballast pieces, so you don't need to do any ballasting.

For a better appearance and sheer adaptability, the flexible track and larger turnouts in both Code 80 and Code 55 offer the best route to track laying. There are medium- and large-radius turnouts, curved turnouts, single and double slips, Y-turnouts, a three-way turnout, crossovers, a scissors crossing and even catch turnouts (to derail runaway rolling stock before it meets the main line). Most turnouts and crossings are available with either insulated or electrified frogs. Once again, foam ballast inserts are available for most of the components if you do not want the chore of ballasting.

The Peco system really is a complete system. You can even get concrete sleeper track, if you are modelling the modern eras. There are also buffer stops, a turntable and inspection pits. Even the track pins and fish plates required for laying and joining track are produced. The dominance of the Peco track system is, therefore, understandable, but good news for the N gauge modeller.

EASITRACK

While not strictly an N gauge product, as it is produced by the 2mm Scale Association for 2mm fine-scale modellers, it is worth mentioning because it

The components of most N gauge track systems tend to be a little over-scale in order to provide a certain amount of robustness. If you want scale-thickness sleepers and thinner rail, you need to build the track yourself, which is really the preserve of 2mm fine-scale modelling. To assist with this, the 2mm Scale Association have introduced Easitrack. Although you build the track, it is a simple case of feeding the rail on to plastic sleeper bases.

is an exciting new development. Although you have to build the track yourself, it's not at all difficult and requires no complicated soldering skills for the plain track. The components consist of moulded sleepers (both wooden and concrete) and lengths of Code 40 rail (either bullhead or flat bottom rail profiles). Simply remove the sleepers from the sprue and feed the rail through the chairs to produce fine-scale flexible track.

It's still early days for the system. No turnouts are available, only plain track, so you either need to connect it to ready-made turnouts, such as those from Peco, or build your own to the same profile. Its advantage is that there is a finer, more true-to-scale appearance to the track compared with ready-made systems, due to the use of the correct sleeper spacing and fine profile rail. Some modellers are very particular about the appearance of the track and they see it as being as important to get it right as you would with a locomotive. If you are a modeller who just sees the track as part of the background scenery, then you are probably best to stay with ready-made track for sheer simplicity.

OTHER TRACK SYSTEMS

It's worth briefly mentioning that there are other manufacturers who make track systems. Some are more comprehensive than others, and some are not widely available in the UK. Graham Farish by Bachmann produce a limited range of sectional track, mostly for the purpose of including within their train sets. Continental manufacturer Fleischmann produce an extensive set of track components, which are ready ballasted. Atlas and Model Power are American companies with a good range of components, including some that are not otherwise available such as a 90-degree crossover.

It is usual, though not always possible, to mix and match track components from different manufacturers' track systems. As long as you use track where the code of the rail is the same (basically Code 80 or Code 55), there should not be a problem. As the rail height is the same, it stands to reason that these track components will be compatible.

The only thing to watch for is the sleeper base, as this is not made to the same exacting specification as

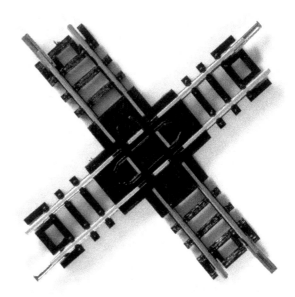

There are several manufacturers of N gauge track and it's worth looking at their ranges, especially for components that are not available from the others. This 90-degree crossing is made in Austria for American company Model Power. It uses Code 80 rail and standard fishplates, which makes it fully compatible with other manufacturers' track.

the rail height. You may find that there is a very slight difference in height between track components from two different manufacturers. If you put a piece from one manufacturer between two pieces from another, the middle piece may float above the baseboard or cause a very slight incline on either side of it. Try running some rolling stock over the track to make sure that this does not cause any problems. If necessary, you can add shims under the track from thin cardboard or even paper, to get everything on the level.

PREPARATION FOR TRACK LAYING

Just like a real railway, you need to consider the foundations on which you will lay your track. In the main, this is going to be some kind of wood-based product, such as MDF or plywood, as part of the baseboard. This gives a solid, flat surface on which you can't go wrong, but there are a couple of extra things to consider.

Some modellers like to use an additional base for track laying. Most popular is cork, which is available in thin sheets or thin track widths. This can be purchased with a 'shoulder' or finished by sanding a shoulder onto the edge (the ballast shoulder is the edge of the ballast just beyond the ends of the sleepers that falls away at an angle to assist drainage). Although the cork is thin, it does raise the track fractionally, which means that any adjacent infrastructure, such as platforms, has to be raised accordingly.

Cork also has sound-deadening properties. Most baseboards (unless open-topped) are like an up-turned box and they can act like a drum or a sound box as a model train passes over. If you are using DCC and sound-equipped locomotives, this un-wanted sound can be distracting or even drown out the sounds you want to hear. This is mainly a problem in the larger scales where the models are physically bigger and much heavier, and thus make more noise. In N gauge, you will probably not notice the noise, although with DCC, the sound-equipped locomotives can be quieter due to the physical constraints on the size of speaker that can be fitted. An alternative to cork, purely for sound deadening, is some kind of thin rubber or neoprene sheet; similar materials are sold for use under laminate flooring and often come with a self-adhesive backing.

With all of these sound-deadening approaches, if you apply loose ballast and then fix it in place with glue, the glue can set such that the track, ballast and foundation are one solid mass, which rather counter-acts any sound-deadening properties the foundation may have. If you want a bit of cushioning for sound insulation without all this hassle, consider simply using foam ballast.

If you don't use cork or foam ballast, one final preparation is worth considering before you lay track, if you are going to use loose ballast. The diluted glue used to fix loose ballast will soak everywhere, including into the baseboard. This won't do any harm to most wooden baseboard surfaces, as the diluted glue is usually a woodworking glue anyway; however, so that you need less glue for ballasting, it is worth priming the baseboard surface before laying track. A woodworking or PVA glue is best (you won't actually require this step if you are gluing the track down anyway). Alternatively, use paint, as most emulsion-type paints will seal the surface they are applied to, though make sure you pick a brown or dark grey colour – if any ballast ever comes loose in the future, bright colours, such as white, will stick out like a sore thumb.

SECTIONAL TRACK

If you buy a train set or a track pack, you will find that it contains sectional track. The name is very appropriate since the pieces of track are in sections of varying lengths and radii. The sleepers (and maybe the ballast) are moulded as a fixed, plastic base – it is impossible to alter the geometry of the track components.

The rail joiners will be firmly attached to one rail at each end. This allows the track to be joined and then separated many times, although eventually the rail joiners will start to loosen a little, which occasionally causes a loss of electrical connection between the track sections. All the sectional track components from one manufacturer will be made to a complementary geometry. For example, a curved piece, when used with a turnout, will allow the diverging track to follow the main track in parallel. In this sense, you can't go wrong using sectional track.

Each section of track has small holes in some of the sleepers to accept track pins, so you can quickly and easily attach it to a baseboard. Gently tap the pins into the baseboard with a small jeweller's hammer, making sure that they go in straight (a pair of tweezers is useful for locating the pin into the hole and holding it until it roots into the baseboard). This is easy on a soft baseboard top material, such as Sundeala, but MDF and plywood are much tougher. Lots of short taps are required, possibly supporting the head of the pin with a pair of pliers. If you bend the pin, don't try to straighten it, as a crooked pin may pull the track out of alignment; pull it out, discard it and try again with a fresh pin. Be careful once the head of the pin is nearly touching the top of the sleeper, as you may start hammering the rails. Use a pin punch to drive the pin but don't overdo it – if the pin is too tight, it may distort the sleeper, which can put the rails out of gauge.

Sectional track is held together by metal rail joiners attached to the ends of the rail. Start by bringing two pieces of track together at a slight angle, so that one rail joiner will slot on to the opposing rail, before the other rail joiner does.

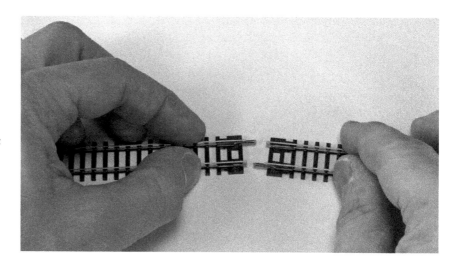

When one of the rail joiners has connected to the other rail, reduce the angle so as to bring the other rail joiner towards the opposing rail.

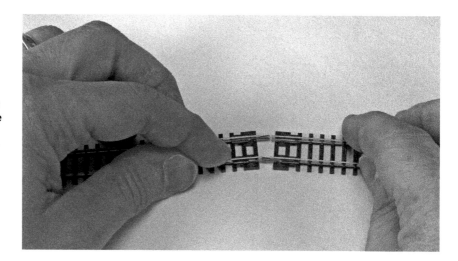

When the second rail joiner has slotted on to the rail, straighten the two pieces and push them together.

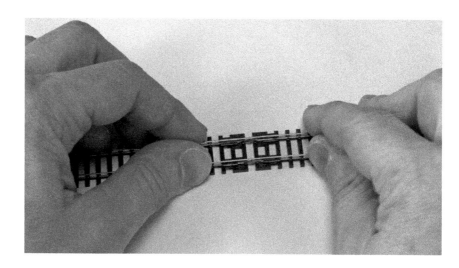

The great thing about sectional track that is pinned in place is that if you make a mistake or change your mind about the track plan, you can pull it all up and lay it again. Don't be tempted to slip a knife under the sleepers and try to lever it up. Sectional track is tough, but you're still likely to damage it unless the pins are in a very soft baseboard material, such as Sundeala. It's better to remove the pin itself. You might just get

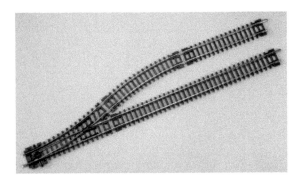

The geometric shapes of sectional track pieces are designed as a whole, so that it is easy to lay track such as these parallel sidings. The single curve piece is the same length and radius as the turnout, so that the S-shape they form automatically returns the diverging track to parallel the main track. Additionally, the single curve and single straight together are exactly as long as a double straight. This is important, since by placing another curve and turnout at the end of the sidings, it would be possible to form a perfect passing loop.

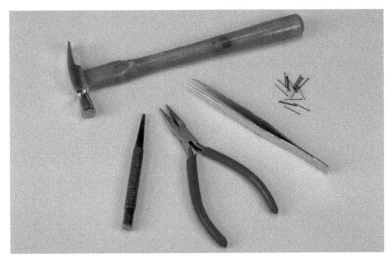

Just a few basic tools are all that is required for laying sectional track – a hammer, pliers, tweezers and a pin punch. Non-magnetized tweezers are an advantage but not essential, as otherwise the metal track pins have a tendency to 'stick' to the tweezers.

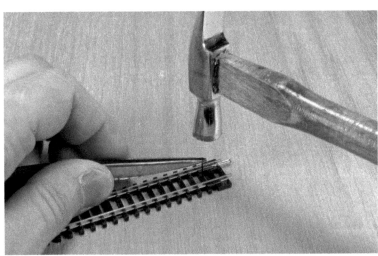

Track pins such as those sold by Peco are very thin ($\frac{1}{32}$in or 0.79mm in diameter), so use a pair of tweezers to hold them while you start tapping them in. It is important to get the pin in at a right angle to the track, as otherwise it can slew the track out of alignment as it is hammered home.

a pair of pliers on the pin head but that's a tricky operation. Instead, use a pair of rounded flush-faced cutters, as the jaws are perfect for getting under the head of the pin. The steel pins are quite hard, so by using only a modest grip, there's no danger of cutting the pin heads off. If all else fails, you can cut the heads off the pins so that the track just lifts off and then you can use pliers to pull the pins out.

Because track pins are so thin, they are very susceptible to bending as they are hammered in, particularly if the baseboard is one of the harder materials, such as MDF or plywood. When you bend a pin, remove it with pliers and discard it – a bent track pin will damage the sleeper or move the track out of alignment. If you keep bending pins, after a couple of taps to get it in straight, change from tweezers to pliers. These enable a firmer grip and, by exerting a very slight upward pressure under the head of the pin, you can counteract some of the tendency for the pins to bend.

Unless you find a tiny jeweller's hammer, the hammer head will not fit between the 9mm gauge of the rails in order to get the pin head flush with the top of the sleeper. Therefore, you need a pin punch for the last couple of taps. Do not overdo it. The pin should hold the sleeper to the baseboard, so that the track does not move up and down when a heavy locomotive passes over. If it's too tight, you may damage the sleeper and distort the track.

If you need to relay the track in another position, use a pair of rounded flush-faced cutters to get a grip under the head of the track pin. You can then draw the pin out fully, or enough to get a good grip with a pair of pliers. Don't reuse the pins, as you will likely have bent them while extracting them.

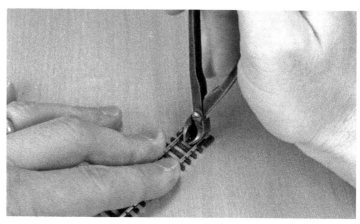

There are thousands of layout designs possible with sectional track but, ultimately, you may find it frustrating by being limited to the set pieces. There is bound to be an occasion when a piece is slightly too long or too short for what you want to do. If you feel that you could do better by cutting up the sections, then you are ready to consider flexible track.

FLEXIBLE TRACK

As you might expect, flexible track can be flexed into any shape you require. It tends to come in 3ft (914mm) lengths, so it's quicker to lay than connecting an equivalent length of sectional track pieces. You can lay it straight, curved, S-shaped or a combination of these and cut it to the exact length that you require. However, this flexibility does require a little more effort to prepare and lay the track.

LAYING FLEXIBLE TRACK

The first consideration is how you are going to fix the track to the baseboard. Unlike sectional track, flexible track does not have any moulded holes for track pins. This is because the flexible track can be cut to any length and the manufacturer would not know where to put the holes in the right place for what you specifically intend to do with the track.

You can hammer a track pin through the middle of a plastic sleeper without having a hole. However, there is a tendency for the sleeper to bulge in the middle to accommodate the track pin. Sleepers in N gauge are not much wider than the thickness of a pin. The best way is to make your own holes in the sleeper. This would be a laborious process using a hand drill; it is quicker (and more accurate) to use an electrically powered modeller's drill.

A Peco track pin is $\frac{1}{32}$in (0.79mm) in diameter; therefore, you need a drill bit of this size. Place the drill bit in the middle of the sleeper and turn the chuck of the drill a few times to start the hole off (if you just switch on the drill, the drill bit can skid off the plastic). Then use the electric drill to go all the way through the sleeper. Make sure to keep the drill as vertical as possible, otherwise the drill may exit the side of the sleeper, not the bottom, and the track pins will go in at an angle. If you still find that it is difficult to get the hole started or in the right place, use a pointed tool, such as a dental probe, to mark the sleeper. The resulting indentation will guide the drill bit through the sleeper to exactly where you want it to go.

Compared to sectional track, flexible track requires more track pins because it is not as rigid. The number of pins you need really depends on what shape of track you are laying. Long, straight runs will

It's hard to go wrong with sectional track but eventually you may find that it feels a little restrictive. Flexible track is not just physically flexible; it offers greater flexibility in how you design and realize your track plan. Forming an S-bend with two lengths of sectional track makes quite an abrupt transition, whereas the one formed below with flexible track is much more subtle and realistic.

You can just hammer track pins through the sleepers on flexible track; however, the sleepers are not much wider than the pins, with the result that the pins tend to cause the sleepers to bulge and distort, as with this example.

When drilling holes for track pins in the sleepers on N gauge flexible track, the drill can spin off the slippery plastic surface (which is not flat, as there is 'wood grain' moulded on the top) or else it can just be difficult to start the hole dead centre. Use a sharp, pointed tool, such as this dental probe, to make an indentation in the correct position into which the drill bit will fit.

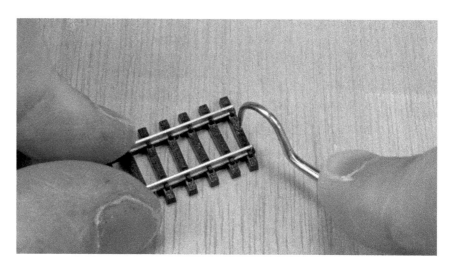

generally hold their shape quite well; a pin every ten or fifteen sleepers should suffice, especially once it has been ballasted. Curves will require a greater frequency of pins in order to hold the shape, the more so the tighter the radius.

An alternative and neater solution to fixing the track is to glue it down rather than pinning it. It's neater because you will not see pin heads on top of the sleepers. These tend to be more noticeable in N gauge because the sleepers are narrower compared to OO gauge or even larger scales. Gluing the track down is a lot more permanent than pinning it down – if you make a mistake, pinned track is easily lifted and relaid.

Most of the DIY-type glues will fix track with plastic sleepers to a baseboard. Grab adhesives that are dispensed from a tube via a nozzle (and have some variation in the name of nails not being required) will work. Be wary of the size of the bead that is produced, since if it is too thick, the glue will ooze up through the sleepers, even above the sleepers. It is better to use a palette knife to smooth the bead before fixing the track on.

The easiest glue for track laying in N gauge is a woodworking glue, particularly a good quality PVA. This can simply be brushed on to the area where the track will go; it can be applied thinly and its drying time allows for adjustment. In all cases where using glue, be aware that some baseboard top materials, such as Sundeala, will soak up the glue to some extent. It is,

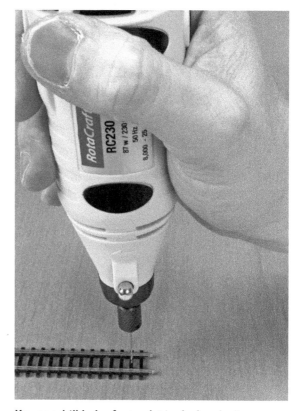

You can drill holes for track pins by hand using a drill in a pin vice but, with every tenth sleeper requiring a hole, it would take you a long time to do just one yard of flexible track. It's a lot quicker to use a mini-drill. If the mini-drill has a speed setting, choose the lowest speed, otherwise the drill bit can melt its way through the plastic as it heats up, rather than drilling through.

The first step in laying flexible track is to prepare the actual piece of track. Cut it to the required length and remove one or two sleepers from the ends that will connect to other track (this piece on Tunley Marsh is the short siding at the end of a loop, so sleepers only need to be removed from one end). Fit track joiners to the already laid track (in this case one is an insulating joiner, so that the siding can be isolated).

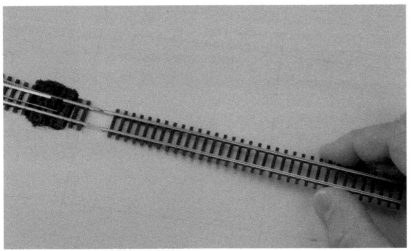

Test-fit the piece of track to check that it is the correct length and that it fits properly into the rail joiners. Slightly elevating the track at the end opposite the join makes it a little easier to get the rails into the joiners. Check that it's straight, either by using a ruler or by eye.

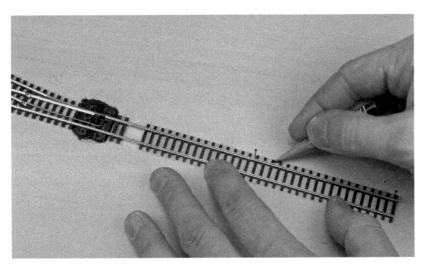

Use a pencil to trace a line around the piece of track; this will be used to define where to apply the glue. Put a track pin at the non-joint end and in the middle; the track butts up to the pins and makes it easy to locate the track while tracing around it, and later when gluing it down, to get it back in exactly the right spot.

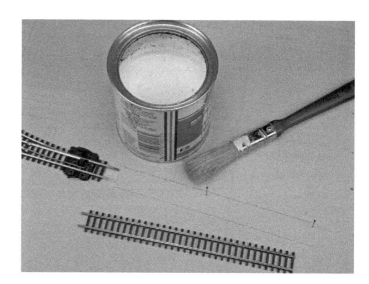

The pencilled outline of the track now gives a clear indication as to where to apply the glue. If your baseboard top is very porous or you are fixing down a very long piece of track, it is worth applying a thin layer of glue as a primer, letting it dry, and then adding a second thin layer of glue to fix the track down. For a short piece like this on a plywood surface, the priming step is not necessary and one application of glue is all that is needed to secure the track.

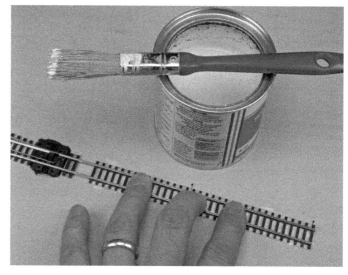

Make sure that the rails are correctly fitted into the track joiners before lowering the track to contact the glue. A quick test is to run your finger over the joint, as the lack of a smooth joint at the top of the rail should obviously alert you to a problem. Most white glues, such as PVA, allow a little time for adjustment to make sure that the track is correctly aligned (check with a ruler or by eye, and make sure that the track butts up to any pins you have used for relocating the track where it needs to go). Once you are happy that everything is exactly as it should be, apply a little finger pressure to fully contact the track with the glue and to make sure that it is level with the baseboard.

therefore, advisable to prime the area where the track will go with the same glue before track laying.

Some track shapes, particularly curves, will need a means of holding their shape until the glue dries. One method is to temporarily pin the track into place; the track pins are not driven all the way home, which makes them easy to remove later using pliers. However, this does leave 'pin holes' in the tops of sleepers, although they may not be noticeable once the track is ballasted and weathered. The metal rail in flexible track gives it a certain amount of springiness; when it is formed into a curve, it has a natural tendency to want to spring back towards a straight shape. This is

not a problem if you are pinning the track down as you go, but it's an issue if you want to glue the track down, as unless you use a contact adhesive that sets immediately, the track will move before the glue sets.

The solution is to put pins on the outside of the rail, on the side that is the outer edge of the curve. The track will naturally push against the pins and, by putting a pin between every five to ten sleepers, you will be able to retain the shape. Add the pins and shape the track, then remove the track, apply the glue and replace the track. Sometimes you may find that you need to place a little weight on the track to make sure it adheres perfectly flat to the baseboard.

To stop flexible track springing back from curved to straight while the glue sets, add track pins on the outside of the radius (against the side of the rail, not through the end of the sleepers). This also allows the track to be removed while glue is applied to the baseboard and then returned to exactly the right place. When the glue is dry, the pins can easily be removed.

For double-track lines, once you have laid one track, you can use that as a fixed point for laying the second track. Peco produce a '6ft way gauge' for this and it's a useful little tool, which is, of course, set to their track geometry (both sectional track and flexible track).

Flexible track is, of course, flexible, sometimes when you do not want it to be. To ensure that straight track is indeed laid straight, place the edge of a steel ruler against the edge of the rail. Of course, you cannot use a steel ruler on curves; however, there is a tool that will do the same job. This is a Track-setta gauge, which is available in a number of common radii. The gauge sits between the inner faces of the rails and holds the track to shape while you fix

LEFT: It is important to check that parallel tracks are indeed parallel and Peco sell a simple little tool to help (for use with their track systems). It is being used here to check that two sectional track sidings are parallel. Note the two tabs on top, which are closer together; these are for use with flexible track where the gap between tracks is more prototypically closer.

BELOW: Flexible track can soon lose its shape, so it pays to check that it is straight when you come to lay the straight lines. This needs nothing more complicated than a steel ruler gently pressed into the web of the rail. If you need to lay a lot of long straight track, it may be worth investing in a yard-length (1m) ruler.

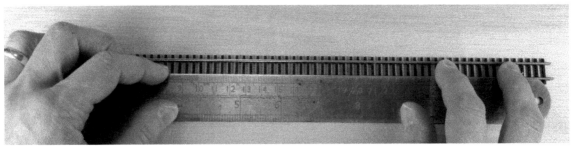

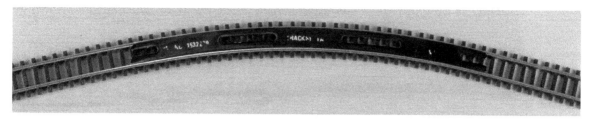

The metal rails in flexible track can be shaped to quite a tight curve but they have a tendency to want to return to a straight shape. In order to both hold the track to a curve and also to get a perfectly even curve, use a Tracksetta. They are available in a wide range of radii to suit most track plans.

the track in place. The gauge has slots in the middle through which track pins can be tapped into holes in the sleepers. If you wish to glue the track, the Track-setta gauges will not be long enough (unless you buy enough of them) but you can still use just one to set the curve and add pins on the outside to mark where the track will go. It's worth noting that Peco's Code 55 rail generally holds its curved shape without re-course to Tracksetta gauges or pins, due to a portion of the rail being buried in the sleeper base, which gives it greater rigidity.

CUTTING FLEXIBLE TRACK TO SIZE

The great advantage of flexible track is that you can cut it to any length required and there are a number of ways to do this. The oldest method is to use a hacksaw, usually the smaller 'junior hacksaw' type. The rule of thumb for cutting metal with a hacksaw is to have at least three teeth on the blade in relation to

the thickness of the metal being sawn. For N gauge rail, this means that you need a fine-toothed blade.

Hold a straight piece of wood at a right angle across the track to guide the blade; if you need to cut a lot of track, it is worth notching the wood to corre-spond to the rails, so that it holds its place a lot more easily. Saw through both rails at the same time, ensur-ing that the cut is as straight as possible. This is easy to do on straight track, but a little trickier on curved track (unless the track is pinned down) because the curvature makes the inner rail shorter than the outer rail. Using a hacksaw works well enough, but it is a little slow. You have to be very precise about where you cut, as it's much harder to take an additional small amount off for adjustment.

A slightly quicker method is to use a carborun-dum slitting disk in a rotary tool (basically a miniature drill for hobbyists that is capable of rotating at much higher speeds than an ordinary drill). The first and

A junior hacksaw is a simple tool for cutting flexible track to size. Use a block of wood as a guide to make sure that the rails on each side are cut to the same length.

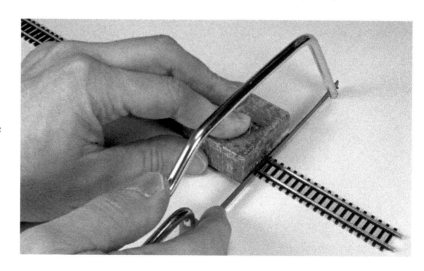

most important point is to use eye protection. The thin carborundum disks occasionally shatter and the very fast rotational speed can spin off the fragments at high velocity. They generally won't do you any harm but if you get a piece in your eye at high speed, it could be a serious injury.

The track needs to be held to stop it moving with the vibration, preferably on a block of wood that raises it slightly to allow good all-round access with the rotary tool. Don't rush the cut and don't press on too hard (which can shatter the slitting disk). Don't be afraid to make the cut in several passes, not least because carborundum is an abrasive material. This means that there's a lot of friction in the cutting process, which can generate quite a bit of heat. Avoid touching the ends for a minute after cutting to make sure any accumulated heat has a chance to dissipate.

It is, of course, impossible to cut both rails at the same time, so you have to be careful to cut them equally. However, the slitting disks do allow very small amounts to be cut off; you can even use the face of the slitting disk like a sander to grind a small amount off the end of the rail. It does take a little practice to get straight cuts, but once mastered, you will be able to cut the track accurately and quickly.

The quickest, cleanest and most accurate solution is to buy a pair of special track-cutters. They look like

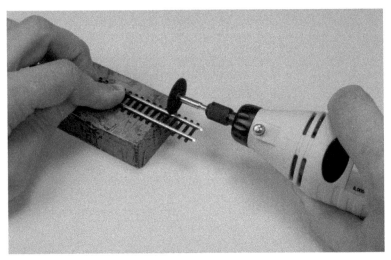

A slitting disk (or grinding disk) is a thin carborundum disk that can be spun at high speed in a rotary tool to cut through one rail at a time. Raising the track on a block of wood keeps it level with the central axis of the rotary tool, so that the cut can be made at 90 degrees. Keep the area to be cut close to the wood as this reduces vibration. Note also how the fingers of the left hand are kept well away from the business end of the rotary tool – it's unlikely to cause serious harm but it pays to play it safe.

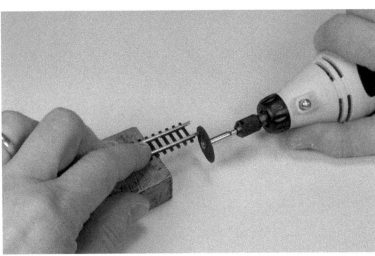

A slitting disk has an abrasive face as well as edge, so it can be used like a vertical sander. This is useful for removing very small amounts off the end of the rails, cleaning any burrs from the cutting process or correcting any cuts that did not go through at 90 degrees.

Special track-cutters are the quickest and cleanest of all the methods of cutting flexible track. The straight face (here, facing the sleeper) will give a clean cut, while the rounded face gives a rougher cut – so remember to get them the right way round for what you want to cut. Always wear eye protection, as when 'nibbling' off a small piece (like in this view) the offcut can shoot off in any direction at incredible speed.

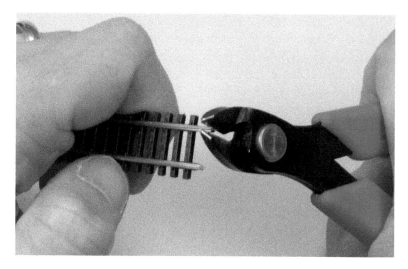

Whether you use a hacksaw, a slitting disk or track-cutters, each will leave varying degrees of small burrs on the end of the rail. Inspect the rail ends for burrs; even if none are visible, carefully run a finger over the end to feel for any irregularities. Use a file to clean the ends of the rails and remove the burrs.

a pair of pliers but they are specially designed to cut all types of rail cleanly and accurately. They are inexpensive (the price of a couple of wagons) and with careful use they will last you a lifetime. It's important to note the two faces of the cutter – one side will give an almost perfectly clean cut, while the other produces a slightly rougher cut. You need to remember to place the 'clean' face against the end of the rail that you want to keep, with the 'rough' face against the end that is discarded as the offcut.

Once again, it's impossible to cut both rails at once; however, the clean cutting face tends to be on the straight side, so you can place a block of wood over the track where you want to make the cut. The cut-

ters can be held against the wood to ensure straight cuts on both sides of the track. Track-cutters are accurate enough to nibble small amounts off (though not as small as is possible with a slitting disk).

It's essential to wear eye protection when using track-cutters to remove any piece of rail not attached to sleepers, as the offcuts can 'ping' off in any direction at an astonishing speed – they won't hurt you but one in the eye could be a serious injury. Don't be tempted to use the track-cutters to chop up anything else, otherwise you will damage them. They are designed for the slightly softer metals used in rail, such as nickel silver, rather than the harder metals like steel.

All of these track-cutting methods will leave small burrs on the end of the rail where it has been cut. It is important to use a fine-toothed file to remove these. If the ones at the top of the rail are left, they may cause the wheels of rolling stock to 'bump' over them. Worse still, they may scratch the wheels. The ones at the bottom of the rail need to be cleaned or else it will be difficult to get the rail joiners on. Both of these problems will be more acute in N gauge, as the rail size is smaller, so any burrs will be relatively bigger.

JOINING FLEXIBLE TRACK PIECES

Having cut the flexible track to the desired length, you will want to join it to other pieces of track. This may be a turnout, or another piece of flexible track, or even a piece of sectional track. Just like the sectional track, flexible track uses exactly the same type of rail joiner (sometimes called fishplates) to join the rails.

Real railways join lengths of rail using a small plate with four bolt holes that is called a fishplate. Model-railway fishplates are a different design but they do exactly the same job – join the rails and hold them in alignment. They are flat on the bottom and curl up and over on top to match the profile of the bottom part of the I-shape of the end of a rail. Model rail joiners perform one additional function, which is to pass electrical power from one length of rail to another.

A rail joiner is basically an interference fit over the end of a rail. As a result, it tends to be difficult to manufacture them to a perfect tolerance every time.

Some can be a very tight fit, while others can be a loose fit, occasionally even a sloppy fit. It is important that the interference fit is just right. If it's too tight, you have to force the rail joiner on to the rail, which can damage or distort the track. If it is too loose, the track may not hold perfect alignment or may not conduct electricity adequately. Any burrs (or removal of burrs) can alter the profile of the rail, which will also affect the fit.

Start by test-fitting the rail joiner on the two pieces of track that you wish to join. If it is a tight fit, try fitting it to a short piece of scrap rail, as this can widen the rail joiner at the top. If it is too loose, very gently nip it at the top with pliers, but not too much or you will distort the rail joiner. It can help to use a file to round off the bottom edges of the end of the rail where it slots into the rail joiner.

Never be tempted to use too much force to fit a rail joiner or to tap it on with a hammer. The rails of flexible track can move within the chairs that hold it to the sleeper (that's how it can bend to any curve). If the rail joiner is stuck on the end of the rail, tapping the rail joiner will tap the rail and can move it through the chairs, wreaking havoc with your track. Even the rails that are more solidly fixed into turnouts can be tapped out of alignment if you are not careful. The best fit is where you should be able to slide a rail joiner on by hand using a small amount of force (maybe a pair of pliers if that helps). If a rail joiner really refuses to slide onto the rail, discard it or try using it later on a different piece of rail that may be more forgiving.

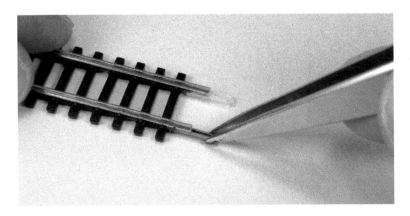

Once any burrs have been removed from the rail ends, rail joiners can be fitted to join to the next piece of track. If the rail end is clean, the rail joiners should simply slide on. This applies equally to metal or insulating rail joiners; one of each type is shown fitted to Peco Code 55 track. It is necessary to remove a couple of sleepers to allow enough clearance for the rail joiners.

Do allow room for expansion, particularly if you are laying the track in a cold room, such as a shed in the middle of winter. There's a temptation to butt rail ends very closely, but then any expansion through heat (or even contraction of the wood in the baseboard) could cause the track to buckle. Only a small gap is required, about 0.010in (0.25mm) at each end of the rail. This is hard to measure. A rule of thumb is to use a finger nail. A more accurate measure is to put a piece of 10thou plasticard (which is 0.010in thick) across the rail ends as you push the other track up to it.

One side effect of these gaps is that you get a bit of 'clickity clack' as wheels pass over the track joints. Modern, continuously welded rail has no such gaps (special overlapping expansion joints are used instead) but it is something that is evocative of the steam era. Some modellers have introduced 'sounding', whereby artificial 'gaps' are added to the rails using the edge of a file to nick the top of the rail. These are placed a scale 60ft (18m) apart (to equate to a real 60ft length of rail). Some things don't scale down so well, especially as small as N gauge, and the resulting cacophony could be off-putting. The clicking over a few actual gaps is probably sufficiently evocative.

Some modellers solder the rail joiners to one or both rail ends for solid construction and good electrical connectivity. In most cases, this is a bit belt and braces. The biggest danger here is expansion and contraction; with one long, fully joined piece of trackwork, there is a real risk that any extreme of temperature (hot or cold) could seriously distort the track. Electrical conductivity can decrease over time, as dirt and dust can get into the joints where the rail joiners meet the rails, but it is rare. If it concerns you or may prove to be a problem, it is better to attach a track power feed to each piece of rail that is separated by rail joiners.

One place where it can be useful to solder the rail joiner to at least one rail is on a curve. It is not advisable to join the track on a curve, especially a tight-radius one, unless you really have to. The 'springiness' of the flexible track that makes it want to return to a straight shape can distort the curve where the rail ends meet, even within a rail joiner. This can sometimes lead to derailments. Don't be tempted to use up several small lengths of flexible track to form a curve – always use a complete piece, where possible.

Some curves require a longer length of track than the 3ft (914mm) lengths that flexible track is sold in, in which case a join is unavoidable. If you really cannot avoid the joint on a curve, solder the fish plates to both ends of the rail while the track is straight, effectively creating a piece of flexible track that is longer than 3ft (914mm). Bear in mind that as the track is formed into a curve, the inner rail will actually be a shorter rail than the outer one. The effect of this is to offset the rail joints. However, staggering the rail joints is no bad thing as it avoids all of the forces of the springiness of the flexible track being centred on one specific spot.

Real railways allow expansion gaps when laying track, otherwise the expanding rails can cause the track to buckle. Model railway track can be similarly affected, especially if the layout is located somewhere that is prone to extreme temperature shifts, such as a loft or shed. Simple expansion gaps can be added where track pieces are joined by placing 10thou (0.25mm) plastic card over the fishplates as the track is connected. This leaves an almost imperceptible gap, which is more than adequate for most temperature ranges.

One other type of rail joiner deserves a mention, and that is the insulating rail joiner. This joins the track together but, as the name suggests, it does not pass any electricity. If you are using a DC control system, you will need isolating sections if you are using more than one locomotive on the layout. Being plastic, the insulating rail joiners are much more flexible than the metal ones. This is not a problem on straight tracks but avoid them altogether on curves, especially ones with a tight radius, as the plastic will distort and, unlike metal rail joiners, plastic ones cannot be soldered.

SLEEPERS AT RAIL JOINTS

It is usually necessary to remove some of the sleepers

from the end of the track so that rail joiners can be fitted. When the rails are joined, this leaves a gap in the sleepers. Peco sell replacement sleepers for their track system that have a notch where the chair would be between the rail and the sleeper, in order to clear the rail joiner; these sleepers simply slide into place under the track. They can be glued into place, although gluing loose ballast in place will eventually hold them securely.

Another method is to reuse the sleepers that were removed. It is possible to cut the sleeper into three pieces: a central portion that fits between the rails and outer portions that fit on each side of the track. These can be glued into place and any gaps will be hidden when the track is ballasted.

To fit rail joiners on flexible track will require some sleepers to be removed. Some Peco turnouts come with spare sleepers to fit under the rail joiners (seen on the left), while the removed sleepers (seen in the middle – Code 55 and Code 80) can be refitted by cutting them into three parts (seen on the right) that fit around the rails.

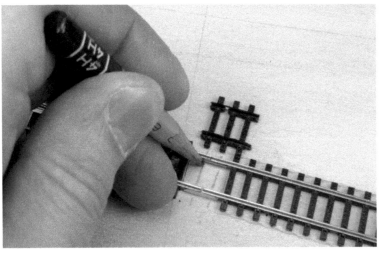

It is important to get the distance between the cosmetic sleepers used at rail joints the same as all the other sleepers otherwise the difference will stand out. Use a spare piece of track or, as here, some scrap sleepers in order to mark with a pencil the required sleeper spacing.

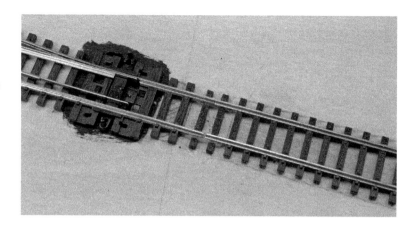

With pieces of spare sleeper glued around the rail joiners, even with this close-up view, it is hard to see where one piece of track is joined to another. Once the track is ballasted and the scenic work is completed, it will be virtually impossible to see the joins.

TURNOUTS

Unless you are sticking with the simple oval of track from a train set, you will need turnouts in order to switch trains to another track or siding. Just like real railways, N gauge turnouts come in different sizes. The larger a turnout, in other words, the longer it is, the greater the radius of the diverging track. The biggest turnouts are called express turnouts, since the gentler radius allows them to be taken at higher speeds. Such turnouts would be unnecessary in a goods yard where shunting takes place at walking pace, and they would take up much needed room.

Turnouts can be a bit of an Achilles' heel for model railway layouts in all scales, since the need to switch from one line to another can cause both mechanical and electrical challenges. By identifying what type of turnouts you require, and with careful installation, there is no need to worry.

TURNOUT TERMINOLOGY

The first thing to grapple with is terminology. Modellers may casually mention some or all of these terms and it is helpful to understand them. Some terms are especially important later on in respect of how the layout will be wired.

The end of a turnout with the single track is called the toe. There is usually a main line through the turnout; the other line that branches off (the curving line) is called the diverging line. The actual change of

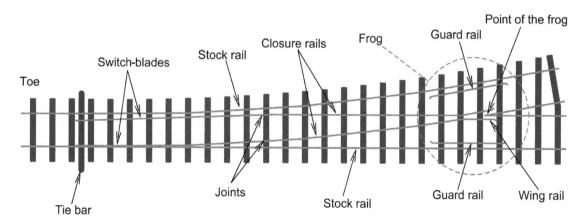

At first glance, a turnout seems to be a relatively simple affair, yet it consists of a number of components and sections. It is worth being familiar with these and their names, both for purchasing and installing a turnout. The diverging line is always the one that curves away from the straight (or main) line. Turnouts are also handed – this example is a left-hand turnout because the diverging line curves to the left when viewed from the toe.

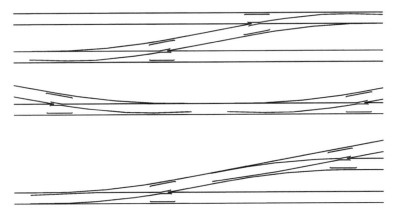

The track arrangement at the top is typical of a crossover between two main lines. In this case, the turnouts are said to be 'facing' and the respective turnout frogs are next to each other. The turnouts in the middle are said to be 'toe to toe', while those at the bottom are in a 'ladder' formation, where the frog of one turnout is connected to the toe of the next. It's useful to appreciate these three possible interrelationships between turnouts, as they can have a bearing on how they are wired for track power.

direction is achieved by the switch; the two rails that move are called the switch rails (or turnout blades). They are joined (and moved) by the tie bar (to which is usually fitted a turnout motor or some other device to switch the turnout). The place where the rail of the main line is joined to the rail of the diverging line is called the 'V' (or 'point' of the frog). This 'V' and the rails that link to the switch-blades are collectively known as the frog (possibly an allusion to the shape of a leaping frog).

There are a number of check rails, which, as on real turnouts, are used to prevent derailments. Model turnouts have a spring under the tie bar, which keeps the switch rail tight against the outer rail. A pair of turnouts where the frogs are next to each other are said to be facing turnouts.

OPERATING THE TURNOUT

The simplest method of operating a turnout is to just switch it by hand. Most turnouts feature discreet handles at the end of the tie bar with which to push or pull the switch rails. Never push or pull the switch rails themselves, as you can damage them. Unless you have a small layout, the chances are that some turnouts will be out of arm's reach. As N gauge is small, you may find it fiddly to operate the turnout by the tie bar, especially if there are platforms, buildings and rolling stock to get in the way. For this reason, some kind of mechanical operation of the turnouts is preferable; besides, hands-off operation looks better without the continual interference in the scene of the 'big hand from the sky'.

Some modellers are put off using turnout motors as it means yet more wiring, but there is a purely mechanical solution. This is called 'wire in tube' and is more akin to the old mechanical operation linked to a lever frame in a real signal box. Quite simply, a wire is attached to the tie bar, which links to a knob at the edge of the layout. You pull or push the knob to pull or push the tie bar. The wire is guided from the edge of the baseboard to the turnout by feeding it through a tube that has a fractionally larger internal diameter than the wire itself. Various crimps can be used to connect sections together, while cranks are available that will even let you go around sharp corners.

This is an old-established method of operating turnouts. There is a certain amount of flexibility with the wire and the tube, such that it can even be made to go round corners. Angle cranks are available if you need to make a sharp 90-degree turn. The tube is usually thin enough to be buried on the top of the baseboard, certainly within a cork sheet top layer, if you use that for sound insulation. An omega loop is usually installed between the knob and the wire in order to absorb any overzealous operation of the knob, so as not to damage the tie bar.

The wire-in-tube method is nice and simple, very robust and requires no electrical wiring. It's perfectly suitable for controlling N gauge turnouts. It does tend to spread the controls out a little, and may not be effective over distances above 3ft (914mm). This will not be an issue on small, portable layouts, although those who prefer all the controls on one central panel will perhaps prefer electrical control (unless you link all the wires into an actual model lever frame).

The most popular means of turnout control is by electrical motors. You can get turnout motors that literally wind the tie bar over but these are overkill

N gauge turnouts can simply be operated by pushing the tie bar over with a finger; however, the size of the average hand in relation to the smaller size of N gauge does mean that it may be awkward to do or that there is a risk of damaging the surrounding scenery.

If you want to control turnouts remotely but think that electrically operated motors could be too complicated for you, consider the ever reliable wire-in-tube method. A strong wire is passed through a tube made from a very shiny plastic tube (the 'slippery' plastic offers less resistance) to the tie bar of the turnout. The tube can be installed above or below the baseboard top. Crimps are used to connect sections together, while omega wires offer a little springiness to absorb any heavy-handed operation. By also connecting the wire to micro-switches or a sliding-type electrical switch at the baseboard edge, various electrical operations can still be carried out such as frog polarity switching or mimic lights on a control panel.

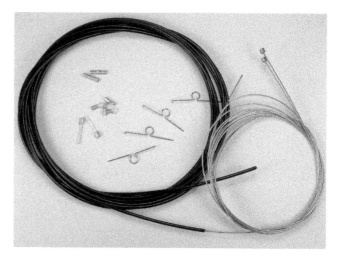

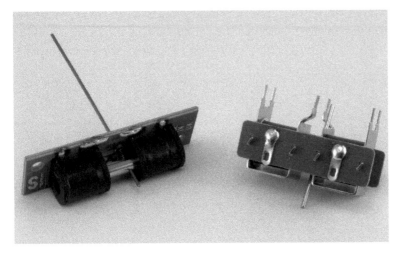

The most commonly used motors for turnouts are the solenoid type, with two electromagnetic solenoids that move a steel bar between them. The SEEP motor on the left has an accessory switch built into it to use, for example, to switch frog polarity; it has to be screwed under the turnout under the baseboard. The Peco motor on the right can have up to two accessory switches fitted underneath and the tabs on top fit into Peco's own turnouts, which makes installation and alignment much easier.

on the small tie bars of N gauge turnouts. Therefore, the usual motor will be the solenoid type. These motors are actually two solenoids, one each side of a bar that is linked to the tie bar. Electrically activating one solenoid attracts the bar and thus moves the tie bar.

Turnout motors, such as those from Peco, can be fitted directly underneath the turnout. The standard Peco motor is quite large in relation to N gauge turnouts, so this can, therefore, require quite a big hole to be cut into the baseboard through which to fit the motor. An alternative, and one required if using the motors from SEEP, is to just drill a hole under the tie bar and feed the actuating pin through the hole to the tie bar. However, it can be difficult to align the movement of the turnout to the movement of the tie bar because they are not joined to each other (such as when fitting Peco motors directly to the turnout).

If you do not fancy fiddling with turnout motors under the baseboard, you can site them above the baseboard and attach them to the tie bar using a linkage (a smaller version of the wire-in-tube method). However, this does require a means of hiding the motor with scenery or under a building (which must be removable for maintenance).

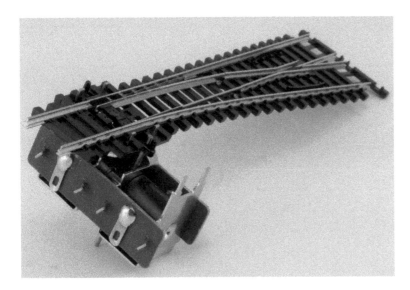

An advantage to the Peco track system is that they sell turnout motors that fit directly under all their turnouts. This means that they are easily fitted and you know that they will work first time, as they are accurately aligned. It does mean that you need to cut a hole in the baseboard surface to fit the motor through. If you don't want to do that, these motors (and others) can be located under the surface with just a hole required for the actuating rod; however, getting this rod accurately aligned can be tricky.

Laying turnouts is largely the same as laying plain track, though if you are using turnout motors, there is a little bit more to it. Start by joining the turnout to the plain track. Apart from curved turnouts and Y-turnouts, they all have one straight edge, which can be aligned to the straight of the plain track. Where the plain track is curved, simply get down and use your eye to check that the line of the track flows smoothly.

When the turnout is properly aligned, hold it in place with a couple of track pins on either side. Decide which side the turnout motor will be; in most cases this does not matter, only where space under the baseboard may be tight. Put a pencil (a thin-leaded propelling pencil, such as used here, is ideal) through the hole in the tie bar on the side that the motor will go. Then manually switch the turnout half a dozen times – this will mark the baseboard with the line that the actuating pin will take.

After using a pencil to draw the arc of the tie bar, it's worth drawing around other areas of the turnout. After removing the turnout, hatched areas at each end of the turnout show where to apply glue when fixing the turnout in place, so as to stay well clear of the turnout's moving parts (if you are using track pins in pre-drilled holes, this is not necessary). Draw around the square base that supports the tie bar and also the four slots through which the turnout motor is fixed.

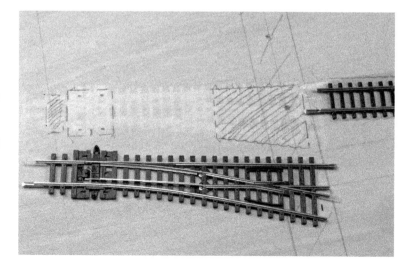

The slots for the turnout motor mounting are now joined into a longer line, which matches the bracket on the turnout motor. On the side of the turnout that will have the actuating pin, this line additionally has some squares drawn on, because the inner brackets on the Peco turnout motors are kinked.

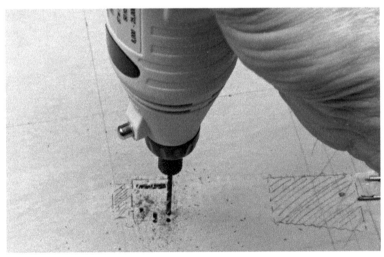

With all the slots marked out, it's time to open them out. Drill a series of adjacent holes along the marked lines, which can then be joined together. It does not need to be too neat as it will be covered by the base of the turnout.

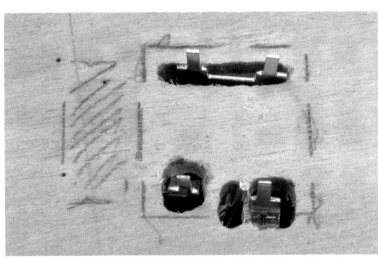

Test-fit the turnout motor into the slots by holding it in place under the baseboard. The slots can be made larger than is needed, which gives some useful 'wriggle room', making it easier to fit the motor to the turnout. Some modellers simply cut a large rectangular hole in the baseboard to achieve the same result; you may have to do this if the baseboard material is much more than about ¼in (6mm), although it does leave a large hole under the turnout through which some light may show.

Refit the turnout in place – the pencil lines will help you to get it back in exactly the right place, as will the holes for the track pins that will temporarily hold it in place. Fit the turnout motor to the turnout to test that the slots in the baseboard are where they need to be. Then switch the tie bar a couple of times to make sure that the actuating pin from the turnout motor moves freely in the slot in the baseboard. If anything does not fit or feels too tight, remove the turnout, enlarge the slots, and repeat this step.

Once the turnout motor and turnout have been tested and work correctly, remove them and paint the square under the base, where the slots are, with black paint. This is because this area is far too small to ballast (which would interfere with the tie bar anyway), so black looks better than bare wood.

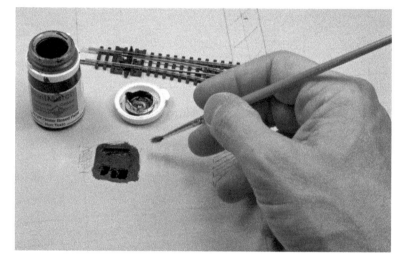

The turnout can now be permanently installed. If you are using pins, put one through a pre-drilled hole in the second sleeper in from each of the three ends. For gluing turnouts, brush a thin layer of PVA into the hatched areas, which are away from the moving parts of the turnout.

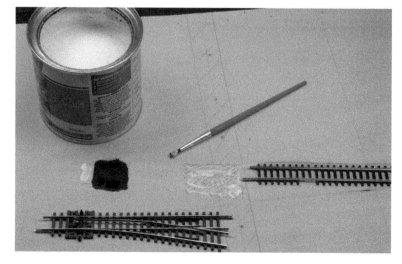

The white PVA glue that can be seen will eventually dry clear. Use a ruler to check that everything is straight. The turnout is held down on the right-hand side by virtue of being joined to existing track. To keep it down on the left-hand side, the track pins have been bent over the rail. Once the glue has dried, they can be pulled out with pliers. The turnout motor will be permanently fitted after it has been wired.

JOINING TRACK BETWEEN BASEBOARDS

If you have a permanent layout, you can treat the whole layout as one giant baseboard and simply run the track over any baseboard joints. If, in the future, you need to separate the baseboards, it is possible to cut the rails and rejoin them later with rail joiners. Portable layouts, which will have the baseboards joined and separated on a regular basis, need a more robust solution.

The simplest approach is to use rail joiners to join the track where it ends on one baseboard and starts on another; however, even using precise pattern-makers' dowels for alignment, it is very difficult to line up the rail joiners when rejoining the baseboards, especially in N gauge. An easier method is to just butt the rails at the joint. To do this requires the track to be located very solidly and precisely indeed at the baseboard edge.

The track can be securely glued or pinned down at the baseboard joints but, as the track is held in plastic chairs moulded on to plastic sleepers, there is still a chance for some slight movement of the rails. It is better if the rails themselves are securely fixed to the baseboard, and the securest means of doing this is to solder them on. Of course, you cannot solder a rail to a wooden baseboard top, but you can solder it to something that is itself securely located in the wooden top.

The simplest anchors for the rails at the baseboard edge are flat-headed brass screws. These can be finely adjusted to the height of the rail by a quarter-turn clockwise or anticlockwise. Make sure you use proper brass screws, rather than brass-plated screws, in order to achieve a solid, soldered joint. Make sure that the screw heads are as level as possible. It is worth drilling a pilot hole for the screws, as it is easier to get this straight with a drill than when trying to just screw into the wood.

For a robust joint between the tracks on different baseboards, you need a means of firmly securing the rails, so that they do not need additional alignment from fishplates. Start by screwing a piece of copper-coated paxolin strip to the baseboard edge where the track will go.

The track leading to the baseboard edge has been glued down (the two track pins are to maintain alignment while the glue sets). The sleepers have been removed where the track goes over the copper-coated paxolin. The track is over-length for now, as it is easier to cut back later, rather than trying to get it perfect at this stage. Leaving the sleepers on the ends of the rails helps to keep them in gauge. This is Peco Code 55 track, so the rail has a deeper profile than the height of the paxolin strip; therefore, it is necessary to file away the underside of the rail until the track fits over the paxolin strip without lifting.

The copper-coated paxolin strip looks extra shiny in the middle because it has been cleaned with a glass-fibre burnishing brush to remove any tarnish – clean surfaces are essential for successful soldering. Plenty of heat is required, as the rail acts like a heat sink and can draw the soldering iron's heat away. Solder has been applied on the outside of the rails, which then flows under the rails. Applying solder on the inside might cover the profile of the rail, which could derail the flanges on rolling-stock wheels.

The copper coating on the top of the paxolin strip will electrically bond the two rails, which would cause a short-circuit. In order to break the electrical connection, use a needle file (in this case a triangular file that has a well-defined edge) to remove the copper coating between the rails. It is only necessary to file a small notch, enough to break the unwanted circuit.

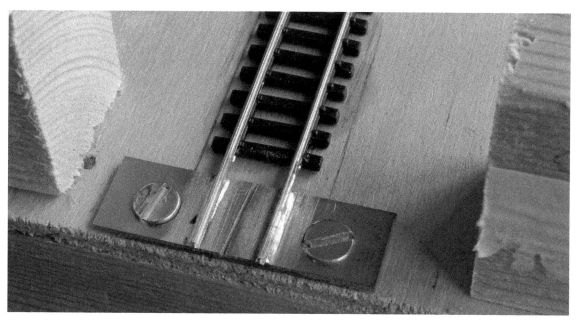

This is the completed track at the baseboard edge. The excess sleepers have been removed and the rails have been cut back so as to be flush with the edge of the baseboard. Note the notch filed between the rails on the copper-coated paxolin strip. Once painted with dark weathering colours, the join will be less noticeable, especially as, in this case, it will be underneath a bridge (the supports for which are the wooden blocks at the side).

The most popular method is to use copper-coated paxolin, which is normally used in the construction of electrical devices. This is available in thin strips, which can be cut to the desired length. Cut a piece about three times the width of the track and then drill holes at each end so that it can be screwed to the edge of the baseboard where the track goes. Being copper-coated, it is very easy to solder the rail to it (use a glass-fibre burnishing brush to clean both the copper and the rail, as cleanliness is a key ingredient for a good soldered joint). Cut a notch in the copper between the rails, otherwise you will electrically join the positive and negative rails and get a short-circuit. If you have multiple tracks crossing a baseboard, simply make the copper strip as wide as the number of tracks, though remember to cut a notch in the copper between each and every rail.

CHAPTER FIVE

CONTROLLERS AND WIRING

Once the track is laid, you'll be itching to run some trains. Yet without power to the track, electrically operated trains are going nowhere. You can push some wagons around (indeed, it's worth doing that as you go along to check that the track has been laid properly) but it's not the same as being able to run your first train. With just the track down and no ballast or scenery, the layout will look a little bare; however, this is the most sensible stage in the build cycle to do the wiring, in terms of access and any fault-finding.

Surveys of railway modellers suggest that wiring is the area that they have the most difficulty with. These challenges are mostly the same in all scales, with very little that is specific to N gauge. Most layout wiring is actually quite simple. Possibly the difficulty is that there can be lots of it. By being organized and understanding a few simple concepts, wiring a layout should not present any difficulties. Like the philosopher who says that a long journey starts with a single step, so the wiring of any layout starts with a single wire. Subsequent wires are merely added one at a time.

Don't be tempted to buy one big reel of the same-coloured wire for all turnout, power and isolation wiring. Instead, buy smaller quantities of different

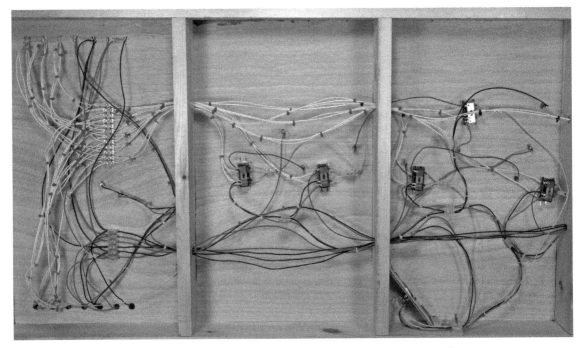

At first glance, this view, under the baseboard of Tunley Marsh, may look like the sort of daunting spaghetti that makes many modellers wary of wiring. On closer inspection, it can be seen that it is neat, tidy and organized. The wires are colour-coded: red (positive rail at the front); black (negative rail at the back); green (common return on turnout motor); yellow (rear solenoid of turnout motor); white (front solenoid of turnout motor); brown (power feed for frog). Paired wires are held together with cable ties (with the excess of these neatly snipped off). Screw terminal blocks are used to join wires together.

coloured wires. By colour-coding your wiring with different colours, you immediately know what type of wire you are looking at (be it power, turnout, etc.). There are no standard colour schemes; it is entirely up to you what you choose, but once you have decided, stick with it all the time.

It's a simple matter to make your wiring neat and tidy so that it is easy to understand what goes where in the future should a fault arise. Where two wires are related (such as a pair going to a turnout motor or track feed), then join them together using cable ties. Write names or numbers next to turnouts or track power feeds under the baseboard, then use the same identifiers under the control panel where the switches are. Try to cut wires to the appropriate length. A little bit of slack allows room for working with the wire, but not so long that the excess gets in the way or hangs down under the baseboard, where it may get snagged and damaged.

Wiring generally falls into two broad areas – that which is required to get power to the track to drive a locomotive, and that which is required to power accessories, such as turnout motors. Only in respect of electrified turnout frogs do the two interrelate. For many years, there was only ever one type of control (DC) but now there is DCC and that's something that needs to be assessed up front.

DC OR DCC?

The traditional type of electrical control is referred to as DC (Direct Current) or analogue (since it is not digital). By simply supplying a varying 12v current to the track, a motor in a locomotive can be powered and controlled. Its simplicity lies in the fact that it cannot do anything except control one locomotive at one time; its complexity is that additional controllers and section switches are required if you want to control more than one locomotive (referred to as 'cab control') or even simply have more than one locomotive on the layout at any one time.

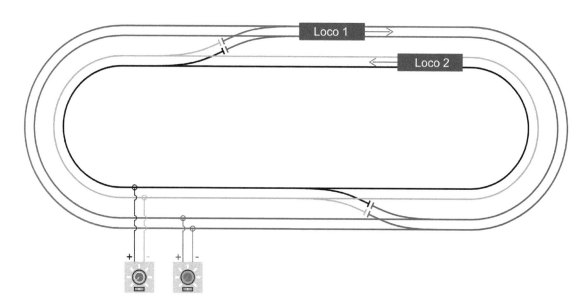

This diagram illustrates a simple layout wired for DC control, with an inner loop and an outer loop. To control a locomotive on each loop requires a controller and power feeds for each loop, and only one locomotive can be controlled per loop. Facing turnouts have been included on the diagram to cross from one loop to the other. They are shown as isolated from each other for simplicity (with self-isolating insulated frog turnouts this would not be necessary). To drive a locomotive from one loop to the other requires both controllers to be set to the same speed and direction.

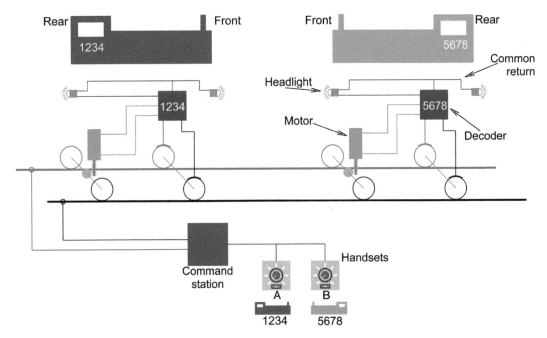

In this diagram, Handset A is set to control Locomotive 1234, while Handset B is controlling Locomotive 5678. The command station interprets what the handsets are doing for their respective locomotives and sends out instructions to the relevant decoder. It's important to understand which end is the front of the locomotive, as this is the end that will go forwards. If both these handsets are set to 'forward', then these two locomotives on the same track will move towards each other.

With DCC (Digital Command Control), all track is live all of the time, so all the wheels on all the locomotives receive the same 16v AC power supply all the time. The DCC decoder in each locomotive takes power and commands from the track and acts like a mini-controller, starting, stopping and changing direction, as instructed. It does this by sending power to the motor. Power is also sent to the headlights; these can be turned on or off by using the handset to send an instruction to the command station, which sends the instruction to all decoders. Only the decoder that it was intended for will act upon it (the decoder itself may be programmed to only switch the headlight on at each end depending on which way the locomotive is travelling).

With DCC, the locomotive has a front and a back, so forwards and backwards relate to the locomotive and not the track. The front is usually the chimney-end, while the back is the cab-end. Diesels and electrics that are symmetrically shaped about the middle, with a cab at each end, usually have a number one and number two end. If you send a DCC locomotive forwards, then pick it up and turn it around, it will still go forwards but that's actually back the way it came.

Each locomotive has a microchip fitted (called a decoder), which is given a unique code number. Only the decoder that matches the code number will follow the commands for that code number. It's a bit like sending a letter to every house in a street, but only the house that matches the address is allowed to open the letter and act on the instructions that it contains.

It's not really practical to operate DC and DCC on the same layout, unless you use totally separate tracks. Therefore, you need to make an upfront decision as to whether to use DC or DCC. A layout can be wired for both systems – simply swapping the controllers and locomotives will allow you to operate one or the other. You may choose to build a DC layout now but it's worth bearing in mind what a DCC

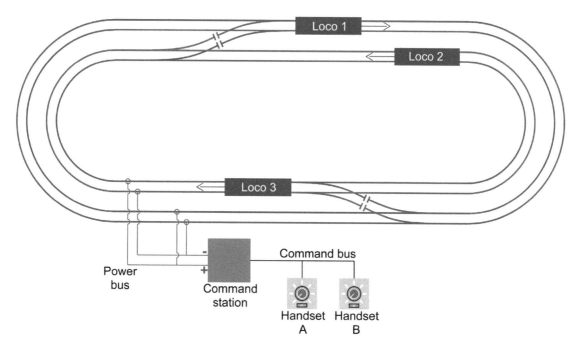

The simple layout with an inner loop and an outer loop is now shown wired for DCC control. Once again, the facing turnouts of the crossovers are isolated from each other for simplicity (not required for insulated frog turnouts, but definitely required for electrified frogs). There is now just one controller (the command station) and all the rails are powered from the same positive/negative supply wires (called the power bus). The 'user interface' consists of a series of handsets that are connected to the command station via a command bus (shown as a single wire, since proprietary cables are available with standard plugs and sockets). Handset A could be set to switch between controlling Loco 1 and Loco 3, while Handset B could control Loco 2. Using separate handsets for Loco 2 and Loco 3 is a good idea as it can be seen that DCC allows them to travel towards each other on the same track on a collision course.

layout requires, as you can build it in now in case you decide to swap to DCC in the future.

These DCC requirements mainly relate to turnouts and the need for extra power feeds. DCC uses more power as it needs to power several locomotives that can be moving on the same track at the same time. It is usual to run power wires around the layout (called the bus wires) of a higher-rated cable from which feeders to the track are taken every yard (metre). Turnouts require that electrified frogs are isolated from adjacent rails.

POWER TO THE TRACK

Any model railway that uses electrically powered motors needs power from a controller to be supplied to the track. On a very simple layout, such as the basic track from a train set or track pack, this can be as simple as just two wires, one to each rail. More complex designs will need additional power feeds. Also, long layouts will benefit from additional power feeds – nickel silver rail is a good conductor, but a long piece of rail is also effectively a resistor. Wherever two tracks are joined with fishplates, there is a potential for a drop in current or even a complete loss, so the best belt-and-braces approach is to add a power feed to each separate piece of rail.

Commercially developed sectional track systems usually come with some kind of power feed that clips to the track. These are satisfactory for getting started but they don't always provide the security of a soldered joint, and they can be a bit ugly and intrusive,

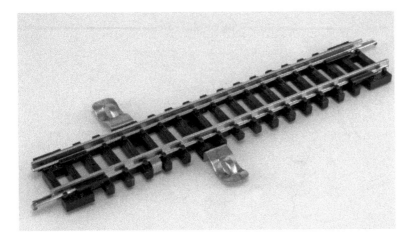

The easiest way to get power to the rails is to use power clips as supplied in train sets and train packs; these clip under the track and touch the rail – no soldering is needed, even the wires from the controller can be simply crimped into the other end. They are, though, rather prominent in any scenic sections, and by being a touch joint not a soldered joint, there is a chance that dirt and tarnishing will compromise the electrical connection over time.

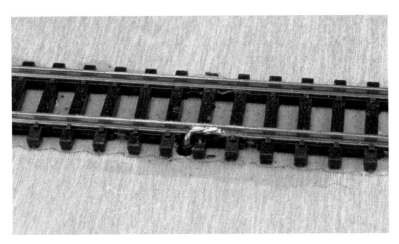

It's fairly simple to bring a wire up through a hole in the baseboard and solder it into the web of a rail. Unfortunately, there's no disguising the wire sticking out from the side of the rail, even once the track is painted and ballasted. This piece of Code 55 rail has a wire soldered to each rail. Quite a bit of heat is required (the rail acts like a heat sink) as witnessed by the slightly melted webbing between the sleepers on both sides.

especially in N gauge. The most robust solution, and the least visible, is to solder wires directly to the rail.

The biggest challenge to doing this in N gauge is that, of course, the rails are quite small. Code 55 rail is just 0.055in (1.4mm) high. The greater the length of rail, the more it acts like a heat sink for soldering. These factors combined can make it all too easy to accidentally melt a few plastic sleepers along the way. It is easier to remove the end of one sleeper, as this gives more room to play with. This piece of sleeper can be glued back in place once the wire is attached (it may need to be trimmed back a little to allow for the wire). Effectively burying the wire in a sleeper helps to hide it, which is important given the smaller size of N gauge, where wires will be all the more obvious.

You only need fairly small-gauge wire for power feeds. This can be brought up through a hole in the baseboard next to the rail. Strip the insulation off the end of the wire and then tin it. Tinning is the process of adding solder to the bare end of a wire to then make it easier to solder it to another wire. The wire can be bent to 90 degrees, so that it sits in the web of the rail (the groove on the side between the top and bottom of the I-shape). This provides a good contact with which to solder the wire to the rail. Use a glass-fibre burnishing brush to clean the side of the rail (any dirt will inhibit the flow of the solder).

An even neater solution is to use 0.5mm brass wire. If you plan where your track feeds will go before you lay the track, you can use a carborundum disk to put a notch under the rail. When the track is laid, drill a hole next to the notch. Feed the wire through the hole – the tip of the wire can be bent to 90 degrees and turned under the rail, so that it rests in the notch under the rail. Once this joint is soldered, it will be very hard to detect, especially once the track is painted and ballasted.

If that seems a bit fiddly, an alternative is to touch the wire to the rail and solder it in place – a small blob of solder is less obvious than a wire soldered to the rail. If you end up with too much solder on the rail, you can use a file or a carborundom disk to carefully reduce it. It's even neater with Peco Code 55 track, since part of the rail is hidden below the sleepers anyway.

'Droppers' are thin wires that take the power to the track and they are much more discreet than simply soldering wires to rails. A feature of Peco Code 55 track is that about half the profile of the rail is hidden within the plastic sleeper base. Use the tip of a sharp knife to cut away this plastic between two sleepers to reveal the rail. A pencil mark between the sleepers is helpful for indicating where the wire feeder will be fitted.

Drill a ⅓₂in (0.5mm) hole through the baseboard top next to the rail. By holding the drill bit against the rail, you will get the hole as close as possible to the rail.

The 0.5mm brass wire for droppers now needs to be fed through the hole next to the rail. The wire will be a tight fit, so use pliers to carefully push it into and through the hole. Hold the wire near to the bottom or it will bend. Once the end of the wire appears under the baseboard top you can use the pliers to pull it through.

Bend the end of the brass wire though 90 degrees and tin it. Tinning is the process of using a hot soldering iron to coat the wire with solder; the resultant coating makes it much easier to solder the wire to the rail.

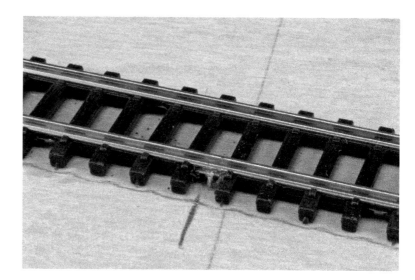

Pull the brass wire through the baseboard top until the end of the 90-degree bend touches the lower part of the rail. You will probably have to nibble back the wire with wire cutters until it fits over the top of the rail. The tight fit of the wire through the baseboard top will now hold it in place.

Solder the wire to the rail for a good electrical contact. The resulting soldered joint may look a little untidy, but it is below the level of the visible rail. Once it is painted and ballasted, it will be hard to spot. If you are worried about melting the ends of the sleepers either side of the joint, cut them off while you solder the wire, then glue them back after everything has cooled.

The final step is to connect the dropper wire to the wires from the controller. You can just solder the wires to the droppers, although there is a slight risk that the heat may unsolder the dropper's joint to the rail. Instead, use brass terminal connectors, having first cut off the plastic insulation. These terminals have two screws – one is screwed to the dropper and the other screw will be used to attach the power wire. This approach also has the advantage that if any alterations or corrections are required to the wiring, it is a simple case of undoing a few screws rather than unsoldering wires.

Needless to say, soldering irons get very hot with a tip temperature of several hundred degrees. Always keep your hands well away from the tip to avoid accidents. Soldering wires to rails can require a lot of heat, as the rail itself acts as a conductor and can take the heat away from the joint; however, too much heat can start to melt the surrounding plastic sleeper base. It requires a careful balancing act and a little practice. Get the hang of it on some scrap pieces of track and when you work on the layout itself, start with the track feeds in places that will not be obviously visible.

WIRING FOR TURNOUTS

The wiring for turnouts is probably as complicated as wiring is going to get. A lot of the confusion relates to whether the turnout frog is insulated or electrified. The so-called 'insulated frog' turnouts are simplicity itself to instal and require no additional wiring. 'Electrified frog' turnouts require some additional wiring and the correct placement of insulated rail joiners, but the additional complexity is worth the effort for better running.

AUTOMATIC ISOLATION

Most commercially manufactured turnouts also feature automatic isolation of the route that is not being taken. This can considerably simplify the wiring required for a layout. Imagine two sidings that stem from one turnout, and each siding has a locomotive on it. Under traditional DC control, only the locomotive on the siding for which the turnout is set can be operated; the other is automatically isolated. This electrical switching is carried out by the switch rails. When a switch rail touches an outer rail (the stock rail), it makes an electrical circuit. A metal-to-metal contact such as this is not a good long-term proposition. Dirt and dust can get in between the touching faces and they are tricky to clean, especially in N gauge.

For this reason, it's a good idea to bypass the isolating switch function of a turnout by adding electrical power feeds to the sidings. If for any reason the electrical contact of the switch rail to the outer rail should fail, the switch rail will still receive electrical power through the frog via the feed to the siding. It might seem like overkill, but a little bit of

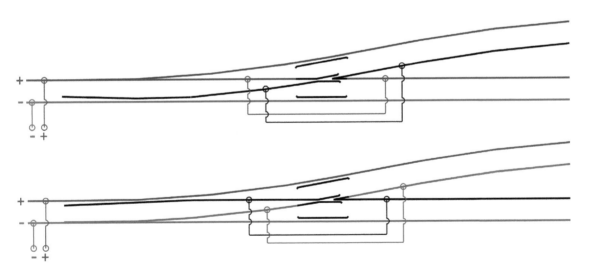

All sectional track and insulated frog turnouts feature automatic isolation of the route that is not selected. This is achieved by additionally using the switch-blades as an electrical switch; however, using a switch-blade as an electrical switch is not a very robust solution and can lead to conductivity problems. Here, the non-energized and 'dead frog' sections are shown in black and change as the turnout is switched from one route to the other. The wiring that bypasses the frog is automatically built into the turnout, so it does not have to be done by the modeller.

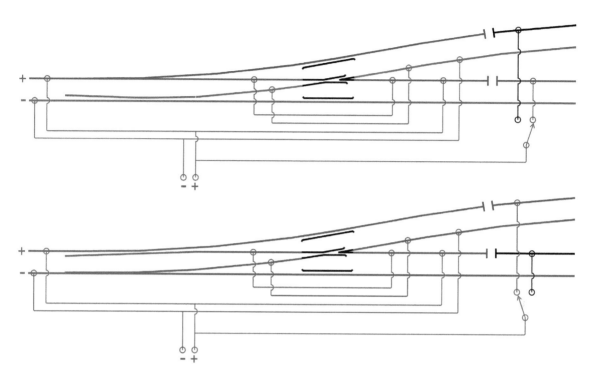

Rather than relying on the turnout's switch-blades to act as a switch, it is better to bypass the self-isolation feature of sectional track and insulated frog turnouts. This ensures an uninterrupted power supply to the switch-blades and the tracks beyond the frog. If the isolation of locomotives is still required, this can be achieved with insulated rail joiners and electrical switches, either one switch per track, or a SPDT (single pole double throw) switch to alternate between the tracks in tandem with switching the turnout. The best solution is to incorporate the switching function with a turnout motor using an accessory switch.

extra wiring at the construction stage will mitigate any potential problems in the future. If you want to be able to park a locomotive on each siding, use panel-mounted switches to energize or isolate the sidings, depending on which way the turnout is set (alternatively, use an accessory switch with the turnout motor to set this automatically).

IS THE FROG DEAD OR ALIVE?

The one part of the turnout that is referred to most is the frog. Unlike real track, in model railways there are two types of frog – insulated frogs and electrified frogs (also known, respectively, as dead frogs and live frogs). This can be confusing to modellers who are new to model railways, but there is actually a very simple distinction between the two types. A dead frog is electrically dead (in other words, insulated). A live frog is electrically live (in other words, electrified).

The electrical power supply to a model railway makes one rail positive and one rail negative. This is fine until two tracks meet at a turnout. Here, the positive rail of one line can meet the negative rail of the other – they meet where the rails touch at the V-shaped point of the frog. With an insulated-frog turnout, these two rails are insulated from each other, so the positive rail does not touch the negative rail at the 'V'. Therefore, an insulated-frog turnout is easy to instal; it automatically protects against any short-circuits.

There is a downside to this simplicity. The frog is made of plastic for electrical insulation, so there is

These two Peco left-hand turnouts may look the same at first glance but the upper one has a dead (or insulated) frog, while the lower one has a live (or electrified) frog. The frog in the upper turnout is mostly plastic, including the tip of the V-shaped point of the frog, so that no rails of differing electrical polarity will touch each other. By contrast, the frog of the lower turnout is all metal and the rails of the point of the frog do touch each other.

now a dead spot in the middle of the turnout. Locomotives with a short wheelbase may become inadvertently isolated on the dead spot (especially if there is some dirt on the track or on some of the other wheels). Longer locomotives (such as steam locomotives with extra pickups in the tender or diesel locomotives with a bogie at each end) are less prone to stalling on the dead spot.

It's a case of 'horses for courses' – a layout with short-wheelbase shunting locomotives means that electrified frogs are a must, while a layout using bogie diesels means that insulated frog turnouts work fine. Many modellers can be put off by the additional complications of electrified-frog turnouts; however, once you understand how they work and interact with the rest of the layout, they are easy to instal. By eliminating the dead spot caused by using a plastic frog, you will improve the reliability of your layout, especially in N gauge.

With an electrified frog, the positive rail meets the negative at the V-shaped point in the frog. A turnout sends a train one way or the other. It follows that sometimes you want the frog to be positive and sometimes you want it to be negative, depending on which way the train is going through the turnout. This 'positive one time, negative another' switch is called the polarity of the frog. In the same way that the switch in the turnout controls direction, as you switch the turnout you want to be able to switch the

polarity of the frog. It is actually a simple matter to tie the two together.

If you are changing the turnout by hand, you can just flip a polarity-changing electrical switch at the same time to change the polarity of the frog. Although you will likely get into a rhythm of doing both operations at the same time, there is still a chance that you will change the turnout and forget the electrical switch, although the resulting short-circuit (if you have a means of detecting that) will alert you to your forgetfulness.

Where the turnout is mechanically operated, it is a simple matter to link the polarity change into the mechanical system. The solenoid-type turnout motors often feature an accessory switch; this is an add-on to the Peco turnout motor, while there is a version of the SEEP motor with an integral switch. Whether using wire-in-tube, a solenoid motor or operation by hand, it is easy to add a separate mechanical link that will operate a micro-switch to automatically change the frog polarity.

WIRING TURNOUT MOTORS

Solenoid-type turnout motors all work the same way. By energizing an electromagnetic coil with a 16v AC supply, a piece of steel can be moved, and by connecting it to the tie bar of the turnout, the turnout blades can be operated. The properties of magnetism mean that an alternating current (AC) powered

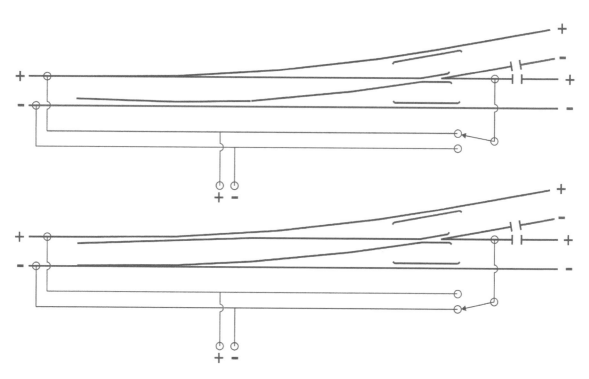

Wiring an electrified frog turnout is initially a little daunting; however, once you realize that the power supply to the frog needs to be switched at the same time as switching the route of the turnout, it becomes easier to understand. The frog and the switch-blades need to be positive (blue) when the turnout is set for the main line or negative (red) when the turnout is set for the diverging line. Note that the rails at the ends of the V-shaped point of the frog are electrically isolated from the tracks that they are joined with in order to avoid short-circuits with any other power feeds. This is not always necessary for DC control but is an essential for DCC control.

electromagnetic coil can only move a piece of steel one way, so turnout motors have a coil at each end of the piece of steel – energizing each coil in turn switches the turnout. Each coil is powered by two wires. One wire is common to each coil (the common return), while the others are connected to an electrical switch.

Turnout motors can be wired back to a control panel, where the switches can be located. There are several ways to operate the turnout. 'Stud and probe' consists of studs on the control panel for each direction of the turnout; touching the stud with a probe completes the circuit. This is a tried and tested method, though it does mean having to hold the probe while you set the route. An alternative is to replace the studs with push-to-make switches; simply

pressing buttons sets the route. Finally, you can use double-pole centre-off (momentary contact) switches, which spring back to a central position. Moving these up or down briefly makes a circuit to operate the turnout motor.

Whatever electrical control method you use for turnout motors, it is worth incorporating a Capacitor Discharge Unit (CDU) in the circuit. This smooths some of the raw power that is unleashed when the circuit is completed to operate the solenoid. It can prevent the action on the tie bar being too vicious, which is important for the smaller workings of an N gauge turnout. It also avoids burning out a solenoid if a circuit is inadvertently made for too long while operating a switch. A CDU will also supply the extra power to operate two turnouts at the same time.

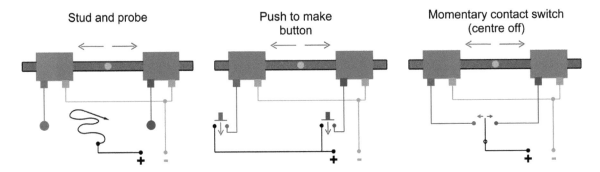

These diagrams show the three methods of operating (and wiring) a solenoid-type turnout motor. The orange boxes are the electromagnetic coils with a steel rod that passes through them; another rod in the middle of this steel rod connects to the tie bar. The green wires are the common return. The red and blue wires complete the circuit on each coil via the relevant switching method (probe, button or switch).

The full extent of a 16v AC power supply can be too much for some turnouts in N gauge, especially if the turnout motor has been designed to be capable of moving bigger turnouts in bigger scales (where the travel of the tie bar is greater). A Capacitor Discharge Unit (CDU), such as this one from Gaugemaster, delivers just the right amount of power to switch a single turnout (or several at once) without fear of damaging turnouts or their motors. Just one CDU is required for all but the largest of layouts, so it is a modest investment for peace of mind.

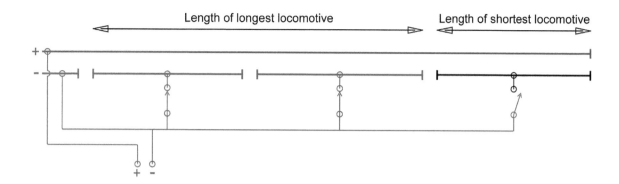

If you need to park several locomotives on the same siding, such as in a locomotive shed, then you will need to use isolating sections. These are simply a break in the rail connected by a plastic insulating rail joiner. Each section requires a power feed, which is easily wired via an on–off switch. Several short sections on one siding allow you to park several small locomotives or a longer one. It does not matter whether you choose to isolate the positive rail or the negative one, but whichever one you chose, be consistent throughout the entire layout to avoid confusion.

ISOLATING SECTIONS

If you want to park a single locomotive on a siding, you could use the automated isolation feature of most commercially available turnouts (although this means relying on the turnout itself for electrical continuity). This won't work if you want to park two locomotives on the same siding, such as you might have in a Motive Power Depot. In such cases, you will need isolating sections to electrically isolate a locomotive. This only applies to DC control systems; one of the advantages of DCC is that it does not require any isolation sections.

The number of isolating sections and where you need them is very much something to determine at the design stage. As you will need to break one rail into two and rejoin the pieces with an insulated rail joiner, you need to know where isolating sections are required before you start track laying. You might be able to cut the track after it is laid, but adding the insulated rail joiner would be virtually impossible.

Each isolating section needs a power feed to be attached. This also needs an on–off switch, so that you can switch the power off in the isolating section when you want to park a locomotive there. You can locate the switch locally to the isolating section, but it is more usual to have all the switches on a control panel. Best of all is a so-called 'mimic diagram' on the control panel, a representation of the track plan, like you would see in a signal box; this makes it a lot easier to remember which switch isolates which bit of track.

CONTROLLERS

Although the motors in N gauge locomotives are physically smaller than their OO gauge counterparts, they are virtually identical from an electrical point of view, unlike motors in, say, O gauge, which are much more powerful and require higher-rated controllers. As a result, there is a wide range of controllers that are as suitable for N gauge as they are for OO gauge. Similarly, most DCC systems work as well with N gauge as they do with OO gauge.

For a DC system, you need to determine at the planning stage how many trains you may want to operate simultaneously. For a small branch-line terminus, this is probably going to be just one train. If you have a four-track mainline oval, you could well be running four trains at once. Each train that is running needs its own controller (a DCC system can control all four trains with one handset, though having more than one handset is probably more convenient).

For a simple DC layout, perhaps just operating one locomotive, a basic controller, such as this one offered by Bachmann, will be quite adequate. All the mains electricity is kept well out of the way by virtue of using a socket-mounted transformer. Unfortunately, there is no 16v AC output, which means that it will not provide power for turnout motors.

Handheld controllers stop you being stuck to one control position on a layout. Additionally, a DCC handset, like this NCE Procab, can be unplugged from one place and plugged in to another using the standard telecoms-type plug on the end of a flexible cord. At first glance, the myriad buttons on this DCC controller may seem confusing compared to a DC controller, but this just allows you to unlock the greater potential of DCC itself.

For larger DC layouts, operating more than one locomotive at once, you will need several controllers. This double-track Gaugemaster DS unit offers two controllers and a 16v AC output from just one mains input (Gaugemaster also offer a quadruple-track unit). The smaller control knobs labelled 'brake' are an additional simulator function that gradually starts and stops a locomotive, rather than having to do that manually via the main control knob.

The simplest controllers are the cased variety. Everything you need is safely contained in one case – one mains wire goes in and a 12v DC feed comes out to the track. You can get double- and even quadruple-track controllers with the requisite number of 12v DC outputs. There is usually an auxiliary 16v AC output to power turnout motors. Cased controllers can sit on a shelf next to a control panel, but on larger layouts you can be rooted to one spot, away from some of the action.

Panel-mounted controllers are literally built into a control panel alongside all the switches for turnouts and isolating sections. These provide a neat presentation of all the controls in one place. A panel-mounted controller will need a 16v AC input from a mains transformer. Never site a mains transformer in the control panel, as it is not safe to mix 240v mains power with 16v AC (a loose mains wire touch-ing a layout wire could send a lethal 240v through the track). Instead, keep it safely isolated in a separate case and simply run 16v AC feeds for the controller and the turnout switches from the transformer case to the control panel.

The most flexible controller, especially if you want to stand and move a bit with your train, is a handheld controller. This is a case that is small enough to hold in one hand, which takes a 16v AC feed from a cased transformer and outputs a variable 12v DC to power the trains. On particularly large layouts, it can be advantageous to have a plug on the umbilical cord for the controller, so that you can plug it in at a number of different positions around the layout. This kind of functionality comes as standard with DCC handsets and you do not even need to stop the train while you unplug and locate to a different position.

CHAPTER SIX

BALLASTING

Since their earliest days, real railways have used stone ballast as a means of both supporting and fixing the track. It provides drainage, holds the sleepers in position and can be graded, packed and tamped to a high level of accuracy to provide a smooth and safe ride for the train. For model railways, ballast does not have to provide any of these functions; it is purely cosmetic, as much a part of the scenery that we are trying to create as trees and hedges. Just like scenery, ballasting needs to look right, and a big part of that is getting the both the texture and the colour just right.

If you had a train set when you were young, you probably just fixed the track down without any ballast. If you used sectional track, which was disassembled at the end of the day, you would not have been able to put on any ballast. Model track without ballast is just about playing trains, which is what you should be doing when you are young or just starting out in the hobby. For a pleasing model railway, you really need to consider ballast. In N gauge, there are three avenues to explore – moulded ballast, foam ballast and loose ballast.

MOULDED BALLAST

Some of the sectional track systems that are commercially available, such as Kato Unitrak, feature a moulded plastic base to support the rails. This moulded base has a representation of the sleepers and the ballast. So at first glance, there is nothing that you need to do once the track is down; in fact, you can keep taking the track up and putting it down and still have ballasted track.

There is no doubt that moulded plastic ballast has some advantages over the other methods – it has greater durability than foam ballast and none of the messiness and tricky application of loose ballast. It has a nicely moulded and consistent 'shoulder'.

There's no getting away from the fact that plastic ballast does look like plastic. It tends to have an even, plastic finish, which does not look like real stone ballast, and if you have two tracks side by side, there is no infill between them. Yet a few simple cosmetic processes will solve these problems. The infill between parallel tracks can be filled with loose ballast; this is

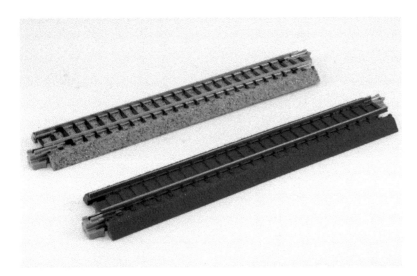

Although the plastic ballast of Kato Unitrack has a 'granulated' finish in terms of texture and colour, in conjunction with the unpainted rails it can seem a little unrealistic. Here are two identical pieces of track but one has been given a single coat from an aerosol can of Phoenix Precision Paint's 'rusty rails' colour (wipe the rail tops with a rag wound around a block of wood immediately after spraying to remove the paint where you don't want it). It's a matter of personal taste as to which one you prefer.

easy to do and, as the loose ballast does not go near the track, there are none of the potential problems of loose ballast.

If loose ballast is used to fill in between two tracks, you will have the colour of the loose ballast and the plastic look of the moulded track ballast, which will look very unrealistic. What's needed is a uniform colour across all the ballast and this is easily achieved by painting all the ballast the same colour. In fact, even on its own without loose ballast, it is worth painting the moulded ballast to remove the 'plastic' appearance.

FOAM BALLAST

This is a type of ready-made ballast that has been around for a long time, referred to as 'foam ballast' or 'foam underlay'. It is made from very lightweight foam that is shaped to the ballast shoulder and to accept the sleepers of the track, so that the sleepers are 'buried' in the foam ballast to a realistic depth. As the foam needs precisely to accept the footprint of the sleepers, it is usually the case that a track manufacturer will also make their own foam ballast to complement their track, although foam components are now available from other manufacturers. It's not just plain track for which foam ballast is available, as the track manufacturers also make 'inlays' for the turnouts as well, so you can use foam ballast for all your track.

Of course, you have to remember to attach the foam ballast before you lay the track. Otherwise, it's very simple and clean to apply. Foam ballast for plain track comes on a long roll, so you just have to cut it to the required length. If you are pinning your track to the baseboard, take care not to tap the pins in too far otherwise you will compress the foam under the track. This would lead to uneven track and then possible problems when running trains. If you do not want to use track pins, you can still use glue. It is best to glue the foam ballast to the track first, and then glue the foam ballast to the baseboard. This can be done with a liberal application of PVA glue.

The sheer simplicity of foam ballast means that it is still very popular after all these years, although there are a number of possible disadvantages to consider. Like moulded plastic ballast, it can look too uniform in colour and unrealistic. In real life, you have to be pretty close to ballast to discern individual stones; from a distance it all looks the same. As N gauge is smaller, this effect, scaled down, is even greater. Some modellers feel that foam ballast just looks like foam; this is true if you operate your trains close up, but from a distance it's hard to tell. Again, there is no infill between parallel tracks, though you can use loose ballast or even more foam underlay to fill the gap. It also raises the track slightly, such that platforms and buildings also need to be raised. Many of these cosmetic issues with foam ballast can, once again, be resolved with a coat of paint.

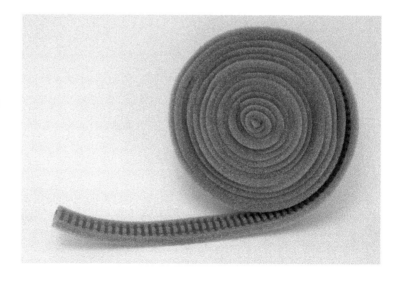

Foam ballast for plain track is supplied on a roll and simply needs to be cut to the required length with a pair of scissors. It is compatible with sectional track and flexible track and the light foam composition makes it easy to shape to even the tightest radius curves. This makes it the easiest and fastest of all ballasting options.

Foam ballast provides instant ballasting. This photo shows Peco straight and curved sectional track pieces pinned to a board using Peco's own foam ballast. The neat ready-formed ballast shoulder is easy to see.

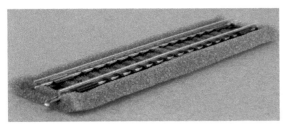

Because foam underlay has a certain amount of natural springiness, it is all too easy to pin the track down too tightly such that the underlay gets squashed. This example has been deliberately pinned as tightly as possible to illustrate the point. Note how the edges of the ballast 'curl up' to reveal a gap underneath and an untidy and random ballast shoulder.

The biggest potential issue with foam ballast is that the foam itself can deteriorate and even disintegrate over time, literally turning to dust. All model railways have a lifespan just like anything (all elements of a model will fade and naturally deteriorate over time). You may even choose to rebuild or start again. Foam ballast should last at least ten years, but if you plan to keep your model railway unaltered for longer than that, do consider that this may be a problem. Anecdotal evidence suggests that the environment can have a lot to do with the rate of deterioration of foam ballast. Places with the potential for wide temperature variations, such as lofts and sheds, may affect it more. The foam itself is lightly porous, so treating it with a wash of dilute PVA and then painting may help to prolong its existence.

TRACK COLOUR

Just like the ballast, the colour of track can vary, usually depending upon use. Real trains generate a surprising amount of muck from the frictions caused by brake shoes on wheels and wheels on rails. Main lines with high-speed trains can be covered in a uniform light-brown colour; goods yards with slow-moving trains can be more subtle.

Brand-new wooden sleepers would have been almost black in the days when they were protected by creosote as a preservative, and most proprietary

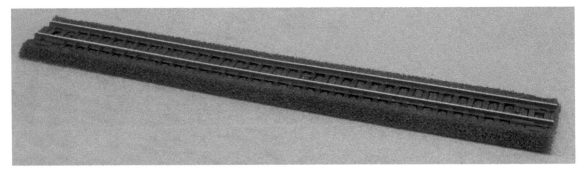

If you think that foam ballast just looks like foam, consider giving it a coat of paint. This is the result on Peco sectional track in the same company's foam ballast after just one pass with an aerosol 'track colour' spray. Everything now has a uniformly dull and dirty colour, which means that the eye is no longer attracted to any sharply contrasting and unrealistic colours.

By far the fastest way to paint the sides of the rails is to spray them with a suitable colour direct from an aerosol. This is best done before ballasting, as the aerosol will otherwise uniformly colour rails, sleepers and ballast. A cloth wrapped around a block of wood is used to clean the tops of the rails to maintain the electrical connection with locomotive wheels. Use masking tape and newspaper to prevent overspray where it is not wanted. Note also the masking tape over the switch-blades of the turnouts – drying paint would likely cause these moving parts to stick together. It is a simple matter to touch up these areas with a brush, though make sure you use a tin of paint from the same manufacturer to ensure consistency of colour.

track comes with the plastic sleepers moulded in black. Over time, particularly as these sleepers were reused in goods yards, they turned to a light-brown, almost grey colour. You can paint individual sleepers with one of a number of commercially available paints that glory in the name of 'sleeper grime'. These are very realistic colours, though painting all the sleepers on a large layout could be akin to painting the Forth Railway Bridge. Modern concrete sleepers start off a very light grey, almost white, and although they weather, the tonal variation is not as pronounced.

In real life, even new rails are rust-coloured, yet almost all proprietary track comes with unpainted rails. Nickel silver is usually used, since it does not rust and conducts electricity very well, but this does mean that you are initially faced with unrealistic ribbons of shiny metal. Painting the sides of model track rails with a paintbrush is as boring as ballasting and may be a little harder with the smaller depth of N gauge rail. Perhaps more than any other job it is an essential step if you are aiming for a realistic-looking layout. Once again, there are a number of commercially available 'rusty rails' paints. It's a hard colour to describe, akin to a light grey-brown. Avoid obvious rust colours, as the end result can look too red or orange.

You can speed things up by spraying the rails. You do not need to own an airbrush as 'rusty rails' colour paints are available in aerosol form. The only drawback is that everything, including the ballast, ends up a uniform colour. This may be appropriate, depending on what you are modelling. The advice here is to look at real railway track, from high-speed lines to slower, preserved railways and see what you want in relation to what you are modelling. Track should never stand out; it should blend into the background, so that the focus is on the trains. An overall colour for rails, sleepers and ballast can achieve this and is the easiest to do with a spray of one colour.

As an overall colour tends to be only applicable to busy main lines, it is usual to paint the rails before ballasting. Spray the track with an aerosol and immediately wipe the tops of the rails with a cloth wrapped around a block of wood to remove the paint where it needs to electrically contact with locomotive wheels. The fine mist of paint from an aerosol applies a thin paint layer – this looks slightly darker on the black sleepers than it does on the shiny rails. You may find that it is necessary to apply a second, even a third, coat of paint. Remember that a better finish will be achieved with several light coats than with one heavy

Apart from a heavily used mainline, where brake dust from trains gives everything a uniform coating, you will probably want to paint the sleepers a different colour after spraying the rails. Weathered wooden sleepers fade from black to a brown colour and this is easily achieved by painting the middles and ends of the sleepers with a suitable colour using a paint brush. Even on big layouts, this is not as arduous a task as you might think. The initially sprayed on colour acts as a good primer to which the sleeper-colour paint will key. It can be thinned slightly with white spirit, so that the loaded brush will easily coat many sleepers at a time.

coat. If you are too heavy-handed with the spray paint, you will get 'sagging', whereby an excess of paint runs or 'sags' down the face of the rail.

If necessary, paint sleepers with 'sleeper grime', perhaps in a yard where there is a more obvious colour difference between the rails and sleepers. Only the tops of the sleepers need painting as the sides and ends will be hidden with ballast. Remember only to paint the 'wooden' part of the sleeper – the chairs that hold the rails will be the same colour as the rail.

LOOSE BALLAST

Loose ballast is not really loose, since it would soon end up all over the place. It is applied in a loose form, and then kept in place with glue. Time and again you will see this referred to in magazines as 'ballasting in the traditional manner', and it is certainly the most popular means of ballasting.

Unlike moulded or foam ballast, this is not a quick method. Nor is it quite as easy. Patience is the order of the day, but this means many modellers think of it as a boring chore. There's no doubt that the finished result is superior to the other methods, especially when viewed close up. It's also potentially much cheaper, so if you don't mind putting some effort in, you can save a bit of money, as well as getting superb-looking ballast.

BALLAST PRODUCTS

One of the biggest problems with ballasting model railways is that it's very difficult to scale down real ballast. If you could pick up a handful of real ballast chips, you would find that they are quite small. Once you scale these down, especially to N gauge, they become no bigger than specks of dust – they would be too small to work with, even too small to see. So selecting a loose ballast for N gauge is a compromise between finding the smallest workable granules and being able to actually discern granularity.

N gauge loose ballast tends to be as fine as it comes; in fact, it is extremely popular with OO gauge modellers as well. There are a number of commercially available loose ballasts from the likes of Woodland Scenics, Geoscenes, Javis and Green Scene. They are usually offered in a range of colours, as the colour of real ballast can depend on the quarry it came from. Most of these ballasts are made from an artificial material for best results. Real stone seems like an attractive option but in most cases it is hard to crush it into sufficiently small pieces without reducing it to dust. It can also change colour quite dramatically when it is glued, particularly slate-based products, which develop a greenish tinge.

A cheap source of ballast that is suitable for N gauge is silver sand, also called agricultural sand. It

A potential problem for loose ballasting in N gauge is to find a ballast material with a granularity that's just right – not so small that it becomes a solid mass when glued, and not so big that it looks like huge rocks. Three of the best materials are shown here (from left to right): Woodland Scenics N Scale ballast; Geoscenes Medium Grey ballast; silver (or agricultural) sand.

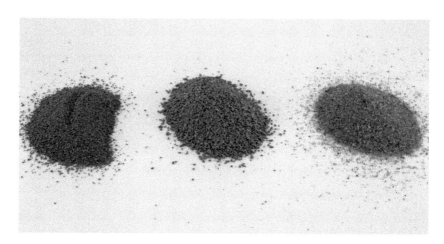

is available from garden centres in small bags; that is, 'small' by gardening standards but huge for N gauge modelling – one bag for a few pounds will probably last you a lifetime. Of course, it is sand, and therefore sand-coloured, but there are various options for achieving a more realistic colour.

APPLYING LOOSE BALLAST

When applying loose ballast, work on small stretches of track at a time. Use a teaspoon to apply a very small amount of ballast over the track, then use your finger to work it between the sleepers. Ballast should come up to the tops of the sleeper and no further, so your finger will remove most of the excess. To get tidy bal-

last, use a soft paintbrush, preferably with long bristles. Brush the ballast at quite a shallow angle so that the bristles move over the sleepers. If the angle of brushing is too acute, the end of the brush will dig the ballast out from between the sleepers. Always brush in the same direction as this moves any surplus ballast along the track to the next section where there is no ballast.

The ballast shoulder is the hardest part to form, as the material is loose; you may find that you need two separate applications to get the correct shape. The shoulder should also be neat. Apply masking tape where the edge of the shoulder will be, so that when this is carefully removed later on, it will remove any stray bits of ballast beyond the edge of the shoulder.

Apply masking tape along the outer edge of the track in order to achieve a neat edge to the ballast shoulder. Where the track curves, use smaller pieces in order to more easily follow the radius of the track.

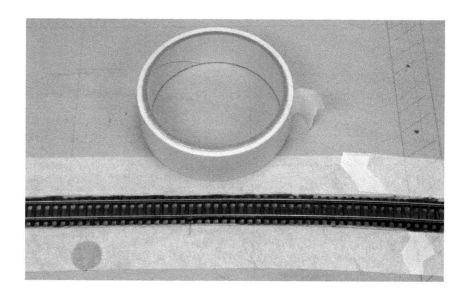

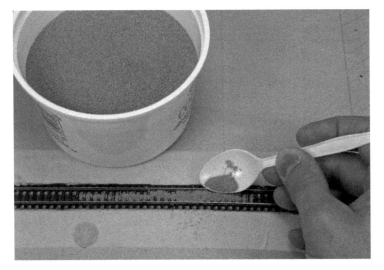

In N gauge, it is very easy to swamp the track with far too much ballast, so start by applying it 'little and often'. Use a teaspoon to apply very small quantities of ballast over the sleepers. You can always add some more, if needed; just sprinkle a pinch of ballast on as if you were adding a pinch of salt while cooking. Note also that the loose ballast has been transferred from the bag it came in into an old food container; this makes it much easier to keep dipping the spoon in and helps to avoid accidental spillage.

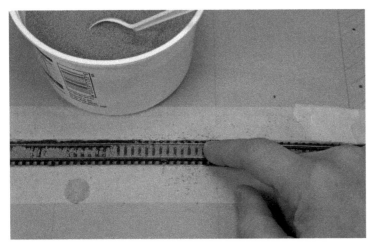

Following the initial application of loose ballast over the sleepers, nothing more sophisticated than a finger is required to flatten it between the sleepers. This will remove any initial excess and highlight any areas where more ballast is needed. The rounded shape of a finger does tend to leave too much ballast at the rail edges, so use a brush instead.

There are a number of ballast-spreader devices available in N gauge, such as this one from Green Scene. They are very useful for quickly applying ballast – an important consideration if you have a very large layout with a lot of track. They need a bit of practice to get the speed right. It is best to move swiftly to reduce the flow or (as here) you can get a bit too much ballast on the track. Even when mastered, a bit of final fettling with finger and brushes is still required.

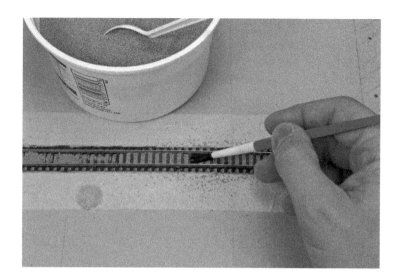

Use a long-bristled soft brush to form the ballast into its final tidy shape, level with the tops of the sleepers and not clogged at the edges by the rails. Always brush gently in the same direction until the ballast is neat and tidy. Look closely for stray pieces of ballast on the sleepers or rails and flick them into place with a smaller brush.

There are a number of ballasting devices now to help with ballasting plain track in N gauge. They are effectively a small box with a hopper inside for ballast and a bottom shaped to the profile of the track. Place the device on the track, add some ballast and then push it along the track, leaving ballast between the sleepers and also a neat shoulder. You need a little bit of practice to learn how to hold the ballasting device and the best speed to move it along the track. Practice first on a piece of track on some newspaper, so that you can collect the ballast and have another go. These devices really do work and if you are building a large layout with a lot of track, the modest outlay will more than repay itself in convenience and speed.

Whichever way you apply the loose ballast, the next stage is to carefully check the ballasting before adding glue. Look for stray ballast granules on top of sleepers, even on the sides of the rail. The latter are important to spot as they could derail a train. Any ballast granules in the wrong place can be coaxed to where they should be by using a small paintbrush. The ballast is now ready to be permanently fixed in place with glue.

FIXING LOOSE BALLAST

The best glues for ballasting are the so-called white glues, such as PVA and woodworking glue. These are water-based and can be further diluted with more water in order to make a liquid mix that will seep

between the small ballast granules. The standard ratio of glue to water is one to one; you will often see this referred to as a 'fifty–fifty mix'.

It's important to add a couple of drops of washing-up liquid to this mix. This is not so that you have sparklingly clean ballast, rather, washing-up liquid contains a surfactant to break down the surface tension of the water molecules (which have a natural cohesivity or 'stickiness'). Without the washing-up liquid, the water molecules 'stick' to each other, and as the glue and water mix is applied to the loose ballast, it can 'ball up' on top rather than soaking in.

An unwanted side effect of using washing-up liquid can be bubbles forming on the surface of the ballast. These usually just dissipate as the glue dries, though the 'popping' of some of the larger ones can dislodge some of the ballast. You can mitigate this effect by using one of the eco-friendly washing-up liquids, since they contain fewer of the chemicals that form the bubbles. An alternative to washing-up liquid is to use a few drops of isopropyl alcohol, which will also break the surface tension of liquids without producing any bubbles.

Another useful step to help the glue and water mix soak in is to pre-wet the ballast. Once again, it is important to add some washing-up liquid to the water to lessen the surface tension. The water is best sprayed on as a fine mist. Garden sprays may not be fine enough, since the water droplets may be large enough to dislodge the ballast granules. Use an atomizer or a fine sprayer instead. Spray the ballast until it is visibly wet and then a little bit more to ensure that it soaks down to the bottom. There is no need to drench it, otherwise the application of the glue will not work.

There are two ways to apply the water and glue mix to the wetted ballast. First, you can use an eyedropper to add drops of glue to the ballast. This needs to be done just above the ballast; any higher and the impact of the drops can displace the ballast, even though it is wet. Second, you can use a pipette to run the glue alongside the ballast shoulder, where it will wick into the ballast. Whichever method you choose, make sure that the ballast is thoroughly soaked with glue.

At this stage, it will look a bit of a mess, as the ballast is drenched, even flooded in places and the white of the glue will show white. Be patient and leave things for a couple of hours, preferably overnight. As the water evaporates and the glue starts to dry, you will be left with just the ballast. Don't be tempted to poke it to see if it is dry – leave it at least twenty-four hours. Needless to say, don't switch the power on to the layout for a couple of days until everything is bone dry.

Loose ballast needs to be wetted or the glue will not soak in properly. As N gauge ballast is very fine, you need a sprayer that will deliver a very fine mist, though like the one shown here, they are very cheap. The white cloud on top of the water in the sprayer is made from the bubbles formed by shaking in some washing-up liquid to counteract the water's surface tension. Note also that the baseboard has been covered with some old T-shirts either side of the track. Although the spray delivers a fine mist, the ballast needs to be thoroughly wetted, and this prevents the adjacent baseboard and electrics being unnecessarily soaked.

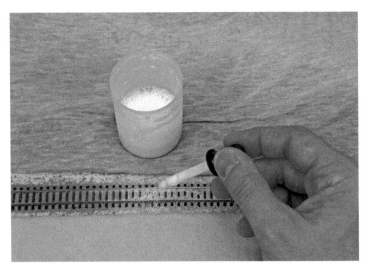

Once a 'white glue', such as woodworking glue, has been diluted half and half with water (and a drop of washing-up liquid added to reduce the surface tension), it will easily soak into the pre-wetted ballast. An eyedropper is a cheap (often free) and easy way of adding the glue. Hold the end as close to the track as possible so that the 'splash' of the falling glue does not disturb the ballast. Don't be afraid to apply plenty of glue, even until the sleepers disappear. Although it will look to be a frightening mess at first, once it has all dried it will look perfect.

A cheap alternative to commercial ballast products is to use agricultural sand, though of course, it is sand-coloured. Such sand has been used on this piece of track. On the left, it has been glued in place with the normal fifty–fifty mix of white glue and water, which has changed the colour from sand to light grey. On the right, some black poster paint has been added to the glue and water mix to give a dark grey, almost black (like cinder ballast), suitable for a goods yard. You can add any colour to any ballast product to get the result you want, and a little variety between mainlines and yards is quite prototypical.

This aerial view of Tunley Marsh shows the painted and ballasted track now complete. The running lines of the main platform, run-round and bay platform use 'fresh' and tidy ballast, while the start of the yard at the bottom-left of the photo uses 'spent ballast', which is darker in colour. All the rail sides have been painted rust colour and all the sleepers are a weathered 'creosoted wood' colour.

There's no such thing as a standard ballast colour, as it all depends on where the stone was quarried. If you are using silver sand, or you don't like the colour of the commercial ballast you have purchased, you can alter its colour during the gluing process. When you make the water and glue mix, add a little bit of poster paint and stir it in thoroughly. Black is a good colour to use, as when it mixes with white glue you get grey. You do have to get the proportions of the mix exactly the same between batches or else there can be subtle variations in the colour of each section of ballasted track.

Once all the glue has set, make a visual inspection of the track for any granules that may have moved to where they should not be, particularly the inside faces of the rails, as this can cause derailments. You'll find that even one granule can be stuck surprisingly fast to a sleeper or rail – the tip of a knife or small screwdriver is usually enough to shift it. Finally, run a vacuum-cleaner over the track to remove any odd, loose bits. This is the ultimate test for your newly ballasted track, as if it survives the vacuum cleaner, you know it will last for years to come.

BALLASTING TURNOUTS

As turnouts are a moving mechanical piece of equipment, you need to take extra care not to gum them up with glue. First, don't add quite as much ballast under the switch-blades – these are slightly deeper than the rest of the rails and adding the normal depth of ballast to the top of the sleeper could interfere with their operation. Second, be extra vigilant for loose granules in the parts that make up the frog, as these will certainly cause derailments. Last, don't be quite as generous with the glue, especially around the tie bar, otherwise you will glue it solid.

It is better to make several light applications of the glue rather than one thorough one, as you would do on the plain track. One final trick is to apply a tiny amount of light lubricating oil to the tie bar and where the switch-blades meet the outer rails. This will act as a barrier to the glue and water mix and prevent the moving parts from gluing solid should you inadvertently apply too much glue.

CHAPTER SEVEN

ROLLING STOCK

While your interest in building an N gauge layout might just be to achieve a scenic masterpiece, for most of us, the real excitement comes when you add the trains. You are most likely interested in real trains and you want to replicate that in miniature. So the acquisition of rolling stock (usually far more than you need) is one of the most enjoyable parts of the hobby.

British outline N gauge has always been relatively well served in terms of the range of ready-to-run locomotives and locomotive kits available, although the quality and fidelity of both often left a lot to be desired. The last ten years have seen the fidelity issues addressed, until now you are hard-pressed to determine whether a photo of a model is N gauge or OO gauge. The range of models has expanded like never before with some ready-to-run locomotives that you would not even previously have expected as a kit.

This chapter includes photographs of some typical examples of N gauge rolling stock from all the major manufacturers of UK prototypes. There is simply far too much rolling stock available to do anything other

than touch the tip of an iceberg. The best advice for anyone new to the hobby, or simply to N gauge, is to purchase all of the fully illustrated catalogues so that you can see everything that's available. If you have a computer, you can usually find this information via the internet. Once you are aware of what's on offer, you can keep track of new releases by buying a regular monthly railway modelling magazine.

STEAM LOCOMOTIVES

Early N gauge modellers of British outline steam railways were limited largely to the products of the Graham Farish factory in Poole. Minitrix did produce a number of British locomotives, although they were usually severely altered in order to fit an existing chassis that was itself from a Continental prototype. The best locomotive of its time was the Peco LMS Jubilee; until Bachmann introduced an up-to-date model of this locomotive, the Peco Jubilees would change hands for exorbitant sums, yet it still passes muster against its ultra-modern replacement.

This Poole-era Graham Farish model is instantly recognizable as an LMS 'Duchess' Pacific locomotive, so although it dates from the 1980s, it's not all bad. The telltale letdowns are the wheels (especially the undersized ones on the bogie), valve gear and cylinders, moulded rather than separate handrails and the lack of cab glazing. However, the body-mounted motor is powerful enough to haul realistic trains. For those who want to improve the model, various detailing packs are available from the cottage industry manufacturers.

The early N gauge steam locomotives usually resembled the prototype that they were meant to represent to varying degrees. What let them down was the level of detail that was possible from a design and production point of view, at a time before computer-aided design revolutionized all manufacturing. Locomotive wheels tended to have extremely unrealistic flanges, emphasized by having shiny rims. The bogies on larger steam locomotives tended to have tiny wheels in order to get the necessary clearance for the cylinders on the curves. Some complex valve gear was produced, although it was untreated, so its shiny surface represented only the best of an ex-works finish.

Some of the small details, such as chimneys and safety valves, were quite crude and all handrails were moulded on to the body, while cab glazing was unheard of.

Despite these faults, they are only faults because there is now a modern generation of models available. The output from Graham Farish, until its sale to Bachmann in 2000, was the backbone of British N gauge modelling. The transfer of production from Poole to the Far East by Bachmann was a protracted affair and the first all-new locomotive, the LNER V2, was largely developed before the move to China. The first all-new modern model was actually to come from a different manufacturer.

Dapol's introduction of the GWR 14xx was the kick-start for a vast improvement in model standards. Its introduction of the BR standard 9F 2-10-0 a few years later gave N gauge modellers perhaps one of the best-ever model locomotives. This example has been factory weathered to a more typically realistic condition.

Union Mills is a small manufacturer who has been producing limited runs of various less common locomotives over many years. This ex-LMS G8 0-8-0 is a typical example. The level of detail may now be considered to be basic by current standards. What has always set these models apart, and therefore made them popular with N gauge modellers, is the enormous haulage capability and reliability of the tender-mounted motor. This model was tested with over forty typical wagons in tow and there was still power to spare.

This ultramodern model of the ex-LMS Jubilee 4-6-0 from Graham Farish by Bachmann is as good as it gets for a model of a steam locomotive. Correct-scale blackened wheels, separate handrails and cab glazing are what we now expect of a model, though this particular example makes for an interesting comparison with the Peco Jubilee produced over thirty years previously.

Dapol was a well-known brand in OO gauge but unknown in N gauge. Its introduction of a model of one of the smallest steam locomotives caused perhaps the biggest event in N gauge in the last fifty years. Dapol's GWR 14xx tank loco might even be considered a little crude by what we have now come to expect, yet at the time it was a fundamental leap in quality and fidelity.

Any new British outline steam locomotive released today will be expected to meet all the following criteria: correct-scale wheels, with thin flanges and treads; see-through spokes and blackened rims; blackened coupling rods and motion; correct profile cylinders; cab glazing; wire handrails; accurate chimney; powerful performance. All these advancements are now taken for granted.

You get an idea of just how small a Terrier 0-6-0T locomotive is in N gauge when you see it next to a ten-pence piece. Incredibly, this Dapol model is fully motorized, and has many separate fittings, such as handrails and glazed cab spectacles. This limited-edition version from Osborn's Models is finished in the GWR livery applied to those locomotives inherited from the Weston Cleveden & Portishead Railway in the 1923 grouping.

Possibly the most sophisticated N gauge locomotive is this GWR 2251 class Collett Goods 0-6-0 made by Peco. It was the first model to come with a DCC decoder already fitted, and it will run on DC or DCC without the need to effect any kind of alterations to the model.

DIESEL AND ELECTRIC LOCOMOTIVES

Not surprisingly, the development of the models of British outline diesel and electric locomotives has followed exactly the same path as that for steam locomotives. To those who think that a diesel is just a box on wheels, there are just as many subtleties in shape and variations in detail as there are with steam locomotives. Since dieselization led to greater standardization, there were fewer classes of locomotive, with the upside that a greater percentage of those classes has always been available in N gauge than would ever be possible with the multiplicity of steam locomotive designs.

Shiny-rimmed wheels with deep flanges were still an issue on early models, as well as some slightly

The class 66 diesel loco is a very modern prototype and it is pleasing that the manufacturers have kept up to date as well. The class 66 model was a curious case of actual competition between two model manufacturers, namely Dapol and Graham Farish by Bachmann, who both produced models of the locomotive. Such duplication is common on the Continent and in North America with their much bigger potential markets, but was unheard of in the UK. It has only occurred once again; many modellers regard the duplication as a wasted production potential for an alternative model. These Freightliner and EWS examples are both original Dapol models.

This Graham Farish by Bachmann class 60 locomotive demonstrates that even on diesels there is a wealth of detail to be included on N gauge models. Of particular note here is the etched side grille, which correctly allows the cooling equipment inside to be seen.

dubious representation of the subtler curves on cabs. Overall, though, diesels and electrics were slightly easier to represent, and some of the original Graham Farish models hold their own against modern models. There is a schedule of replacements with better models, the main advancements being directional head and tail lights (which switch from head to tail when the direction of the locomotive changes), handrails and more powerful mechanisms.

BELOW: *Overhead electric locomotives have not been overlooked by the manufacturers. On the left is a Poole-era Graham Farish class 90 next to a more modern model from Dapol of a class 86. Both wear the triple-grey Railfreight livery with distribution sector branding. This photograph illustrates another interesting aspect of manufacturer competition, namely, subtly different interpretations of the shades of some of the livery colours.*

ABOVE: *It's not just very small steam locomotives that can now be manufactured in N gauge, as this diminutive Class 04 shunter demonstrates next to a ten-pence piece. The model is from Graham Farish by Bachmann and features a working fly crank behind the steps, cab glazing and separate handrails.*

The standard of painting and livery application is much improved as well.

One feature of the so-called standard classes is the number of sub-classes – an extra grille here or a window there. At one time, a model locomotive body would have been 'one size fits all', yet modern production techniques allow for most, if not all, of the body variations to be produced.

Graham Farish did produce a number of 'overhead electric' locomotives for those modelling railways powered from wires supported by catenary masts. Their class 87, class 90 and class 91 have now been joined by Dapol's class 86 model.

MULTIPLE UNITS

Diesel Multiple Units (DMUs) have been a part of the railway scene for over fifty years and, in fact, Electric Multiple Units (EMUs) have been a feature for even longer. The early GWR AEC 'flying banana' railcar was a part of the original Graham Farish range for many years. Yet only one first-generation DMU and two second-generation DMUs were to be produced, despite their modern ubiquity and suitability for small layouts.

Once again, it's so much better now with several quality models of first-, second- and even third-

These superb models of DMUs from Graham Farish by Bachmann represent the first generation (the class 108 on the left) and the second generation (the class 150 'sprinter' on the right). The class 150 has been made available with plain cab as here and also corridor connection cab, an example of the sub-class variants that manufacturers are now able to offer.

N gauge modellers have had to wait a long time for a ready-to-run model of a third-rail EMU prototype. The amazingly detailed 4-CEP four-coach EMU from Graham Farish by Bachmann has certainly been worth the wait. This model first appeared in the Bachmann OO gauge range. Research and drawing accounts for a substantial amount of the development cost of any model in any scale, so manufacturers seek to maximize the return on this effort by producing models in both scales. Therefore, the OO gauge range is often a sneak preview of what will eventually be available in N gauge.

generation DMUs from both Dapol and Graham Farish by Bachmann. The latter have even produced the first ready-to-run third-rail EMU and overhead EMU in N gauge.

COACHING STOCK

Coaches have always come in a huge range of sizes and designs, depending on what they were for, which company built them and what era they were built in. Graham Farish originally made brake and non-brake versions of mainline and suburban coaches to a generic design, which was then released in the livery of each of the big four pre-nationalization railway companies, and even a few pre-grouping liveries (the SDJR versions are rare collectors' items).

Both Minitrix and Lima produced British Railways Mark 1 coaches though to 1:160 scale, which meant that they always looked under-scale. The Graham Farish Mark 1 was quite a decent model for its time. The use of a clear plastic body-shell meant that numerous types and liveries could be printed on to what was prototypically a standard body and chassis. This method did mean that there was no real depth to the window frames, even in N gauge. The later Mark 2, Mark 3 and Mark 4 models were also good representations, especially the bogies, although the lack of any interiors did give them quite an empty feeling, especially on those coach designs with large windows.

The revolution in the production of N gauge models over the last ten years has not just been limited to locomotives. Once again, Dapol started the ball rolling with a superb GWR auto-coach to complement the launch of the 14xx tank loco. Three of the big four's most common coaches have now been introduced (GWR Colletts, LNER Gresleys and LMS Staniers), with just the SR soon to be represented. Bachmann have introduced a brand new Mark 1. The latter is typical of the modern approach in that only a few old-style models are renovated; in most cases it is simpler to start afresh.

WAGONS

The greatest variety of rolling stock is always to be found in wagons, no matter what era you are modelling. The leader in this area was Peco, with a range of good-quality wagons covering a number of types, both old and modern. Many of these models have actually stood the test of time well. Both Graham Farish and Peco understandably used generic wagons to represent the myriad private-owner coal wagons and big four railway companies.

Special mention must be made of the Minitrix Merry-Go-Round (MGR) hopper, probably the finest model of its time and capable of attracting lofty second-hand prices, until both Peco and Graham Farish by Bachmann introduced newer (though only slightly better) models in the last ten years.

The original Poole-era Graham Farish Mark 1 coach model (top) was quite good for its time but it struggles to hold up against the modern model (bottom) from Graham Farish by Bachmann. The relief around the doors and flush glazed windows on the new model is far superior to the printed sides on the old one, although many modellers say that they prefer the roof on the old model.

N gauge passenger trains are finally served by scale-length accurate representations of coaches. Left to right here are: GWR Collett (Dapol); LMS Stanier (Graham Farish by Bachmann); LNER Gresley (Dapol).

The British Railways Mark I coach was a standard design that came in many variations. The new range of models of these ubiquitous vehicles from Graham Farish by Bachmann features many of these variants from brakes to composites and even TPOs (Travelling Post Office coaches). The latter is perhaps the finest N gauge model coach ever produced.

The newest manufacturer of private-owner wagon models in N gauge is Mathieson Models with a superb range of beautifully printed models celebrating the coal-mining heritage of the UK. Of particular note is this manufacturer's decision to use a clear plastic version of the standard N gauge coupling. Opinion is divided as to its merit but there's no doubt that under certain lighting conditions (such as for this photograph) they are less obtrusive than a normal black plastic coupling.

Improvements in recent years, as part of the general raising of all standards of rolling stock manufacture, have been better wheels, more chassis details (such as V-hangers and vacuum equipment) and better livery and lettering application. The modern generation of short-wheelbase, private-owner coal wagons are incredibly authentic and detailed, and yet they are extremely affordable.

The extensive range of wagons from Peco has been a mainstay of N gauge modelling for over thirty years. These examples use a common 10ft wheelbase chassis but there are three different body styles. Peco also produce a range of wagon loads designed to fit their own models.

RIGHT: Dapol's entry into N gauge was inevitably accompanied by a private-owner coal wagon model (bottom right). Dapol have used this basic model for private commissions for as little as 150 examples, boosting the wagon-collecting side of the hobby. They have recently introduced a superior private-owner coal wagon (bottom left) to rival the ones from the other manufacturers, though this one additionally features a close-coupling mechanism. Dapol have not limited their range to the 10ft wheelbase, producing a 20t all-steel open (top left) and a 21t all-steel hopper wagon (top right) on a 12ft wheelbase.

Perhaps the biggest impact has been the noticeable introduction of more wagon types, rather than simple re-liveries of existing models, often representing something that they are not quite right for. Many modellers like wagons because they offer variety, and now the N gauge manufacturers are serving that demand more than ever.

WAGON LOADS

You can never tell with enclosed wagons whether they are full or empty but this is not the case with open and flat wagons. Most railways tried to run their wagon fleets with loads as much as possible, since moving empty wagons around made no money. Railway modellers seem to prefer to model their wagons loaded,

Graham Farish originally produced a rather rudimentary 10ft wheelbase private-owner wagon (top), but the company's sale to Bachmann eventually brought forth a beautiful and varied range of private owner wagons (bottom) using the more prototypically common 9ft wheelbase.

rather than empty, and for this reason, there are a number of wagon loads available for N gauge rolling stock.

Peco make a series of plastic inserts for their wagons to represent coal, crates and barrels. Similarly, Parkside Dundas make a plastic coal insert for MGR hopper wagons. The biggest range of wagon loads is produced by Ten Commandments. These are cast in plaster and cover most ready-to-run wagons. They require painting, but this is a simple matter in most cases; acrylics are best, as a diluted wash can be painted over the plaster, which soaks in for very real effects.

Finally, lots of things that are sold as scenic accessories for layouts would themselves have been transported by train, so make ideal loads. Examples include road vehicles, like cars and tractors, stacks of crates and barrels, pipes and planks – your only limit is your imagination.

Railway wagons don't just come as small private-owner coal wagons – modern wagons are much bigger, as illustrated by this selection of bogie wagons from Graham Farish by Bachmann. On the left is an EWS coal wagon, a far cry from those little private-owner wagons of old.

Tank wagons always make interesting models, so they have been well represented by manufacturers over the years. From left to right: Graham Farish by Bachmann TTA in Shell-BP livery; Peco TTA re-liveried to ICI livery by Robbie's Rolling Stock; Peco 10ft wheelbase tanker (Berry Wiggins, a limited edition for the N Gauge Society); Dapol six-wheel milk tanker in Cooperative Wholesale Society livery.

The most comprehensive range of loads for open wagons of various types is produced by Ten Commandments. These are made from plaster, which is a material ideal for painting with acrylic paints thinned with water, since subtle variations can be made with the same colour, as seen here on the boxes and crates.

KIT-BUILDING

Most of this chapter looks at ready-to-run rolling stock that you can take out of the box and just place on the track. These models are now superb and faithful reproductions of a huge variety of locomotives, coaches and wagons. This variety was not always the case; the range of ready-to-run models was limited, with many key prototypes noticeable by their absence. It's a feature of the model railway trade that there will always be kit manufacturers, both large and small, who will step into any vacuum left by the ready-to-run producers. These 'cottage industry' suppliers have done a lot to support N gauge modelling over the years.

The main producers of locomotive kits were Langley Models and P&D Marsh. These kits were designed to fit the existing Poole-era Graham Farish chassis, which often required some substantial alterations. The kits themselves were made from castings in white metal, a material that is easy to cast and to clean and work with, but can lead to varying levels of quality. A more modern material is casting resin, which allows for some fine detail, although, like white metal, anything that relies on a rubber mould made from a master can lead to variable results.

Coach kits were less common, as it's not easy to make coaches from white metal. Etched brass is usually the material of choice, and mention should be made of the Ultima coach kits, which were manufactured to a high standard in etched brass with white metal details. The Mike Howarth Stanier coach kits were an invaluable base model for many years, until the introduction of ready-to-run models from Graham Farish by Bachmann.

The biggest area for kits in N gauge has always been with wagons. While there are a few white metal and etched-brass kits, the material of choice has always been injection-moulded plastic. A vast array of wagons is available in kit form from the likes of Parkside Dundas, Taylor Plastic Models and Chivers Finelines. The sizeable Parkwoods Models range is now owned by the N Gauge Society, who themselves have by far the single biggest range of kits available.

The popularity and range of kits has been helped by the ready availability of chassis on which to build them. They are mostly manufactured by Peco. Having

This is a kit-built GWR 56xx 0-6-2T locomotive made from a Langley white metal kit. It looks like the prototype, although when seen close-up like this, it looks a little rough around the edges. The Poole-era Graham Farish chassis from a 94xx Pannier tank is all shiny wheels and pickups, which does not help the overall finish.

Most coach kits in N gauge have tended to be from etched brass, which is a difficult medium to work with for the beginner. Thankfully, the N Gauge Society has produced a plastic kit for a Gresley Full Brake, which with care will build into a very good model.

By far the most numerous and popular kits in N gauge are those for wagons. The N Gauge Society has the largest range of kits, many using an existing chassis, such as these RCH 7 plank coal wagons, which use a Peco 9ft wheelbase chassis. The N Gauge Society also exclusively sells the ModelMaster transfers that were used to letter these models for a selection of Welsh collieries.

a reliable chassis on which to build is like building on a firm foundation and it takes away a lot of the difficulty that the modeller would otherwise face. Plastic is by far the easiest medium for the average railway modeller to work with.

CONVERTING TO DCC

Interest in DCC is increasing in all scales around the world, due to the advantages it offers of multiple trains on the same track, finer control of lighting and performance, and of course sound. British outline models have kept pace with this demand and most of the new generation of N gauge models are easily converted to DCC.

Any DC model can be converted to DCC, but with some it is easier than with others. The requirement is to electrically isolate the motor; in other words, you need to put the decoder between the motor and the track (that is, the pickups). Modern locomotive models already have this built-in and are generally referred to as 'DCC ready' (that is, ready to be easily converted to DCC, but DCC is not actually fitted). To run on DC, the electrical isolation is bypassed by a blanking plug – it's shaped like a DCC decoder but all it does is connect the motor terminals to the electrical pickups. By removing the blanking plug and substituting a DCC decoder, you convert the locomotive from DC to DCC – it is as simple as that.

Don't be put off having a go at kit-building in N gauge, especially with wagons. There are some very simple kits available, which are ideal for beginners. The most undemanding of all are from the wide range of kits made by Peco, such as the disassembled five-plank wagon shown on the left. At just nine parts, with no glue required (the body is secured by the two small nuts), it does not get any easier. Just paint the body and add some transfers to achieve a realistic-looking model like the finished one on the right.

The only considerations are to make sure that the decoder you use has the same number of pins as the socket on the locomotive, and that you buy one that is physically small enough to fit inside the locomotive body.

Converting older N gauge models to DCC is more convoluted. In most cases, the pickups, chassis and motor are one integral unit so it is hard to electri-cally isolate the motor. It can be done, but it does require some disassembly and conversion of the chassis, so it's not for the beginner. With the wide range of modern models that are easily converted to DCC, it is quite easy to go the DCC route for control, with some models even offering the ability to support sound.

Most of the new generation of steam locomotive models house the motor in the tender. This is where you will find the blanking plug, which needs to be replaced with a DCC decoder. On this Dapol 9F locomotive, hold the tender chassis with one hand and pull the tender body off.

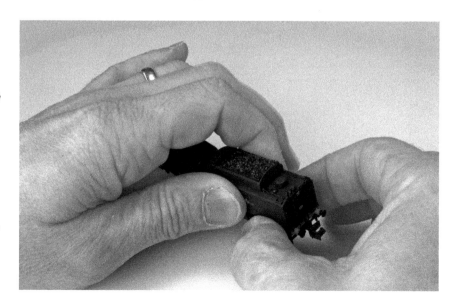

With the tender body removed, you can see the motor (the 'coal' is a separate moulding). The blanking plug is the small circuit-board labelled 'TOP', which is plugged into the socket (the black rectangle at the bottom rear of the motor circuit-board).

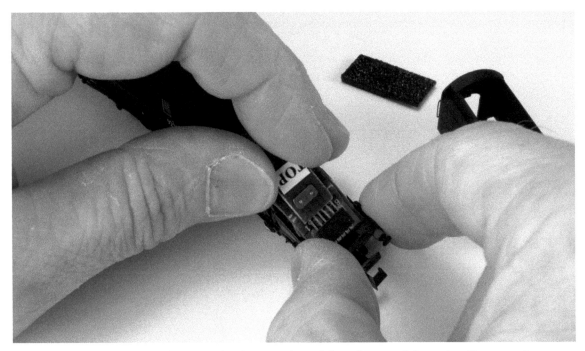

To remove the blanking plug, gently grip the chassis and carefully pull it out of the socket. Always retain the blanking plug in case you ever want to reverse the process and run the model on DC again.

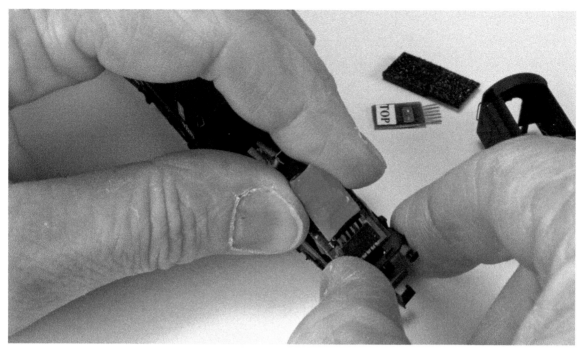

A six-pin DCC decoder is required for Dapol's 9F locomotive. Gently grip the chassis and carefully slide the decoder into the socket.

The model has now been converted to DCC. All that remains is to refit the tender body and test the locomotive with a DCC controller.

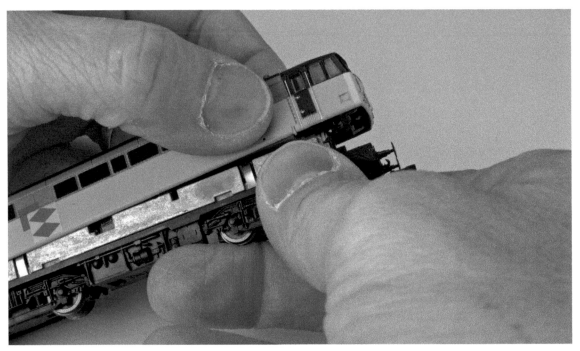

Converting a diesel or electric model to DCC is a virtually identical process as for a steam locomotive. The first step is to remove the entire body, as with this Dapol class 86 locomotive. Grip the chassis and gently pull the body away at one end and then the other.

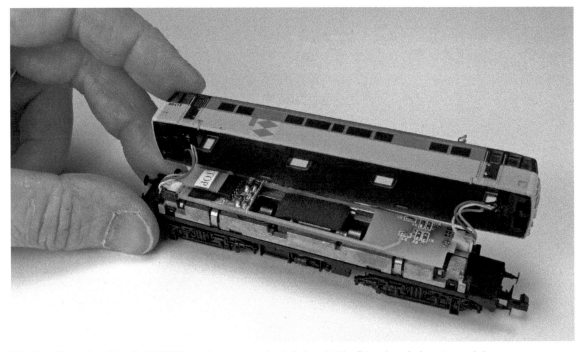

The blanking plug (labelled 'TOP') can be seen at the left-hand side. Diesel and electric models are now usually fitted with head and tail lights, so the body remains attached to the chassis by wires at each end.

The wires for the lights in the body are connected to the chassis by simple plugs. It is easier to disconnect these at the end with the decoder socket for ease of access.

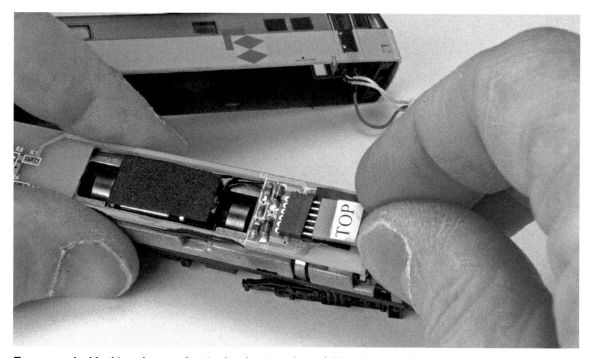

To remove the blanking plug, gently grip the chassis and carefully pull it out of the socket. Always retain the blanking plug in case you ever want to reverse the process and run the model on DC again.

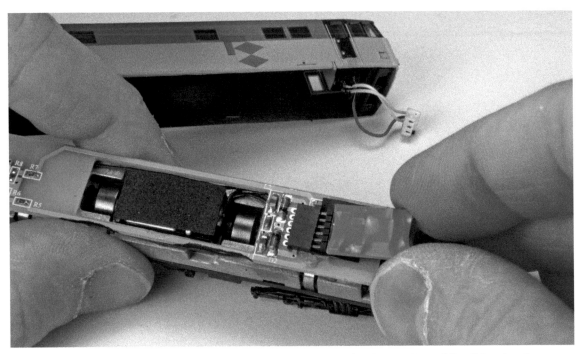

A six-pin DCC decoder is required for Dapol's class 86 locomotive. Gently grip the middle of the chassis and carefully slide the decoder into the socket.

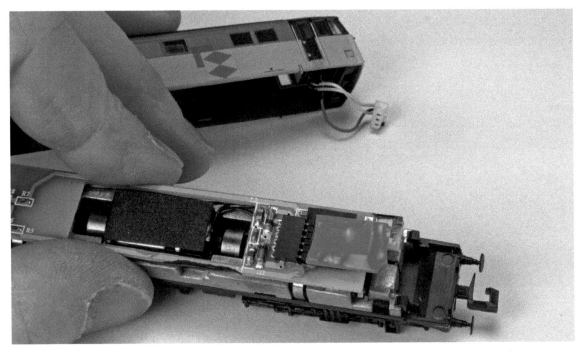

With the decoder in place, the model is now ready for DCC operation. Refit the plug for the wires for the light and then gently push the body back on to the chassis. The model can then be tested with a DCC controller.

CHAPTER EIGHT

COUPLERS

The ability to couple and uncouple vehicles is a fundamental requirement of any railway rolling-stock system, whether real or model. This flexibility allows wagons, even coaches, to be sent down different routes, or simply swapped about for maintenance. A model railway coupler needs to do everything that a real coupler does. In addition, it needs to be reliable and easy to use, as well as being practical in miniature, especially in N gauge. To understand model couplers, it is first of all worth taking a look at real couplers.

PROTOTYPE COUPLERS

From the very beginning of railways, and still today, coupling is often nothing more complicated than a chain from one vehicle that is slung over a hook on another. This allows vehicles to be daisy-chained together for pulling. For pushing (more formally known as propelling), the chains slacken and the vehicles contact each other by means of buffers. Buffer heads are actually quite small, as most real railway curves are quite generous – they are nowhere near as tight as even the most generous curves in model form. Using buffers on models would not generally work as you can get buffer-locking.

Buffer-locking occurs (sometimes even with real trains) on very tight corners, usually on the transition from the straight to the curve. The buffer of one wagon can slip behind and lock itself behind the buffer of the adjacent wagon on the inner radius, as the wagons enter the curve. This is why shunting locomotives have such oversized buffer heads for industrial or dockside areas with very tight curves. Sometimes, the inner radius forces the inner buffers of adjacent wagons together too tightly, enough to cause one wagon to push the other one off the track. It may also happen with propelling moves.

An alternative coupler that started to be used on coaching stock in Britain at the start of the twentieth century was the knuckle coupler. The way they work can be explained by imagining that your hands are the knuckle couplers. Relax your hands and hold your arms so that the knuckles of each hand face each other (with one thumb up and one down). If you push your hands together, the knuckles brush across each other and touch the opposing palms. Now tense your hands and try to pull your arms apart – the fingers of each hand lock together. This is the basic principle behind a knuckle coupler. Moving your wrists so that the fingers move away from the opposing hands allows the hands to be separated – this is how uncoupling takes place. Knuckle couplers take the strain for pulling but they also do so for propelling, so there is no need for buffers (which are either not fitted, or are retracted).

It's helpful to understand real couplings before looking at the model ones in order to assess how each of the model options reflects the real thing.

RAPIDO COUPLERS

The coupling, designed over fifty years ago for the Arnold Rapido products, has become the de facto standard N gauge coupling around the world, so much so that it has given it a name. Its design was copied and spread, becoming the default coupler, perhaps by accident rather than design. If you were designing a coupling system today for small-scale models, you probably wouldn't come up with the same design. It has its advantages and disadvantages, but it's possibly the one element left that has the potential to put people off N gauge.

It is, though, a very simple system. Vehicles are easily coupled as one Rapido rides up over the other. If you lift a vehicle off the track, the couplers simply separate; compare this to trying to untangle OO gauge vehicles fitted with tension-lock couplers.

The Rapido coupler may not look pretty, but its overwhelming advantage is its standardization, which means that it is universal and fully compatible. Nearly forty years separate the wagon on the left from the one on the right, yet they both still couple to one another. From left to right: early Graham Farish (without spring); early Graham Farish (with spring); Peco; Dapol; Mathieson Models; Graham Farish by Bachmann.

Vehicles can be uncoupled by various means. With some dexterity, you can lift one coupler by hand with nothing more than a piece of bent wire. This can be done mechanically via a lifting ramp, which pushes the pin under one of the Rapido couplers, lifting it clear of the other coupler. This same function can be achieved more discreetly by fitting curved metal tails to the Rapido coupler, which hang down to the track.

Rapido couplers are very easy to join, especially on wagons such as these Peco ones where the coupler is not held in place with a spring. The sloped faces of the Rapido allow one coupler to slide over the other.

Once one Rapido coupler has slid over the other, the wagons are coupled together. The Rapido coupler is quite obtrusive on the end of a wagon, but less so between coupled wagons.

Peco sell an etched stainless-steel fret of 'tails', which allow hands-off uncoupling using electromagnets (or permanent magnets) that attract the tail downwards, thus levering the coupler upwards. They are easily separated from the fret with a knife and require nothing more than a pair of pliers to bend them to the required shape. They fit to Peco (and most other) Rapido couplers with just a spot of superglue.

When the metal is attracted by a permanent magnet or electromagnet hidden under the track, uncoupling can be achieved. Sprung couplers usually require the spring to be removed. To stop the coupler from drooping down without a spring to hold it, bend the tail upwards so that it touches the chassis. If this does not work, complete replacement couplers are available from Peco and Dapol. If all else fails, lifting a wagon at one end will separate it from the next.

Simple though the Rapido may be, it is far from perfect. While the basic shape of the coupler is the same from all manufacturers, there are subtle differences in the dimensions used. There can be difficulties coupling up to vehicles from different manufacturers, although once coupled, they are usually fine. Some manufacturers use springs to keep the coupling level; however, these can make the Rapido stiff to operate, sometimes even impossible to couple to the next wagon. The spring does keep the Rapido in place; Rapido couplers that are not sprung can all too easily separate when you don't want them to, causing a train to split.

Drooping is another problem, where a Rapido coupler has not been fitted properly to the model or where the Rapido sticks up. The Rapido coupler has to be perfectly level to function properly. The pin under a drooping coupling can catch on turnouts, leading to derailments. Ironically, the move towards Normal European Modelling (NEM) pockets (which is progress) is also another problem, since the couplers are held more rigidly; they cannot always rise sufficiently to couple to another vehicle.

Love it or loathe it, the Rapido is set to remain a part of N gauge modelling for the foreseeable future. Its worldwide ubiquity and relative simplicity give it a durability that is hard to resist. Yet change is afoot, and there are alternative couplers that are worth considering.

NEM POCKETS

The pocket is the part of a coupling mechanism that actually holds the hook and arm part of the coupler. With Rapido couplers, it can just be a box with a spring to hold the coupler. Without a spring, a deeper box is required that physically holds the Rapido coupler in place. What is common with all of these pockets is that they usually form an integral part of the vehicle. If you want to change the type of coupler, you have to permanently remove the existing coupler pocket. It is a destructive process with no way back

The NEM pocket is a breakthrough for N gauge modelling as it allows couplers to be replaced with alternatives or removed altogether (such as on the last vehicle in a train). No special tools are required as couplers simply pull out of and push into the NEM pocket.

(although you can buy replacement Rapido couplers and pockets from Peco and Dapol). Wouldn't it be simpler if you could just unplug the Rapido and re-place it with a different coupling? If you change your mind, you just swap the Rapido back again.

The Normal European Modelling Standards (or NEM Standards) are a guide for manufacturers with the aim of creating compatible products. They cover many aspects of railway modelling, just one of which is the coupling and the pocket that it fits into. In theory, it should be possible to take a coupling from one manufacturer and fit it into the pocket of a different manufacturer.

Increasingly on N gauge models you can do a non-destructive, fully reversible swapping of couplers, thanks to the introduction of NEM pockets. You can simply pull out the Rapido and replace it with another coupler. Everything is a simple push fit. While everything is supposed to be to the same size, a coupler from one manufacturer can be a tight fit in the NEM pocket of another. This interchangeability is a great step forward for N gauge but the question remains – what do you replace the Rapido coupler with?

DUMMY KNUCKLE COUPLERS

The first alternative coupling to be considered is a dummy knuckle coupler, as first introduced by Dapol.

It's called a 'dummy' because it does not allow hands-off coupling or uncoupling, although vehicles that are fitted can be coupled together to form fixed rakes. If you are running fixed rakes that never change, the dummy knuckle coupler is a great alternative, as it is a vast visual improvement and it is quite discreet.

The Dapol version supplied with most of their rolling stock is available in short-shank and long-shank options. This allows the distance between vehicles to be varied depending on how tight the curves are that will be used. Two long-shank couplers give plenty of distance between vehicles. Two short-shank couplers get the vehicles very close indeed. A long-shank coupler on one and a short-shank coupler on the other allow a distance somewhere in between.

MICRO-TRAINS KNUCKLE COUPLERS

The Micro-Trains knuckle coupler was originally an N gauge version of the Kadee coupler in HO scale. The latter company sold the N gauge version and the Micro-Trains company came into being. Although it is an American product with American rolling stock in mind, it can be used on British outline rolling stock.

Unlike the dummy knuckle couplers, the Micro-Trains product is a fully functioning knuckle coupler.

Here are three Dapol bogie china-clay tankers, each fitted with a different coupling. The one on the left has the standard Rapido coupler; the one in the middle has Dapol's long-shank dummy knuckle coupler; while the one on the right has Dapol's short-shank dummy knuckle coupler.

Vehicles can be coupled by simply pushing them together – the knuckles slip over each other and firmly couple together. Uncoupling is achieved by using magnets – these form a magnetic field that attract the trip pins on the couplers in opposite directions. The movement of the pin opens the jaws of the coupler in a prototypical manner. The vehicles can then be uncoupled.

There's another trick up the Micro-Trains coupler's sleeve. Most hands-off uncoupling devices in most scales mean that vehicles must be left wherever the uncoupler is. The Micro-Trains coupler is what is known as a 'delayed action' coupler. Once the couplers are separated, the magnetic field continues to hold the jaws apart. Bringing the vehicles together brings the couplers into contact again, but this time (with the jaws being open) the outer edge of one open jaw fits into the other, preventing the knuckles from coupling. This means that the vehicles can be propelled away from the magnet. When the vehicle is positioned where required, the other vehicle is drawn away without the need for uncoupling. In other words, the uncoupling was 'delayed'.

This is a hugely flexible system and great fun to operate, although it's worth pointing out a few disadvantages for the British modeller. Once again, conversion to Micro-Trains couplers is a destructive process, as the couplers are a complete replacement. Despite the spread of NEM pockets on newer models, Micro-Trains have not yet made a coupler that is compatible

This is an illustration of the difference between using standard Rapido couplers (top) and replacement short-shank dummy couplers (bottom). The dummy couplers are far less obtrusive while bringing the wagons significantly and more prototypically closer.

with these pockets. When purchased individually or in small packs, the Micro-Trains couplers are expensive. This is all right for a small layout with limited stock, but less so for large collections, never mind the work involved in installation. A cheaper alternative is to buy the Micro-Trains couplers in kit form. They are tricky to put together at first, but once you have the hang of it, you can produce them quite quickly.

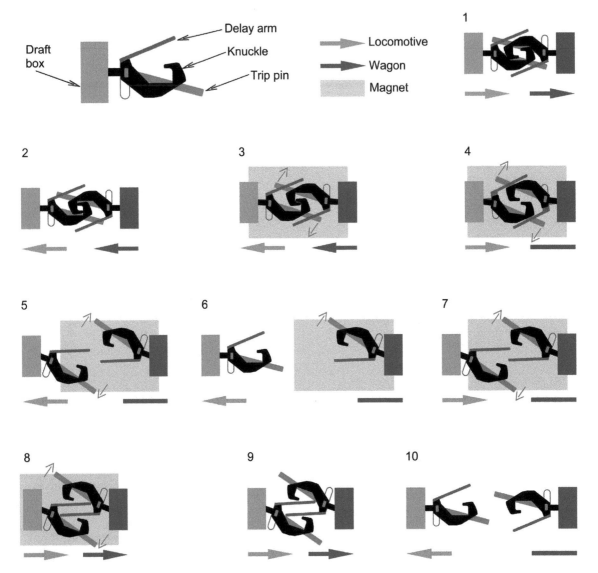

The Micro-Trains coupler is a miracle of miniature engineering. Viewed from above, the trip pin is attached to the knuckle, passes through the delay arm and then loops under the knuckle. The 'draft box' is an American term; it is basically the box that holds the knuckle and the delay arm, and a spring between them. *1.* The couplers in 'compression', where the locomotive is propelling a wagon; the opposing knuckles press on the delay arm. *2.* The couplers in 'tension', whereby the locomotive is pulling the wagon; the knuckles hold each other like hooks. *3.* What happens when the locomotive pulls a wagon over a magnet – the trip pins are attracted outwards by magnetic force, but the hooked ends of the knuckles hold the couplers together. *4.* The locomotive moves back over the magnet but the wagon stays still. The couplers move from tension to compression but before they can compress, the magnet pulls the trip pins outwards, which opens the knuckles. *5.* The locomotive moves off the magnet – with the knuckles open, the wagon is left over the magnet. *6.* The locomotive moves all the way off the magnet, whereupon its knuckle is returned to the normal position by the spring in the draft box. *7.* The locomotive returns towards the wagon; the magnet again moves the trip pin, thus opening the knuckle. *8.* The two couplers are brought together, but this time, with the magnet moving both trip pins outwards and thus opening the knuckles, they cannot couple. Instead, the delay arms move inside the knuckles. *9.* The locomotive having propelled the wagon off the magnet, the delay arms prevent the knuckles from coupling but allow the wagon to be propelled. *10.* The locomotive reverses again but it leaves the wagon where it is required, and both couplers return to the normal position.

Fitting a Micro-Trains coupler in place of the normal Rapido coupler requires a bit of work and is usually a non-reversible process. This is the underside of a Dapol open wagon showing the traditional N gauge couplers retained by springs inside the pockets. The first step is to disassemble the wagon – use a small screwdriver to gently lever the wheels from between the W-irons and remove the body by pressing the brown retaining lugs at each corner.

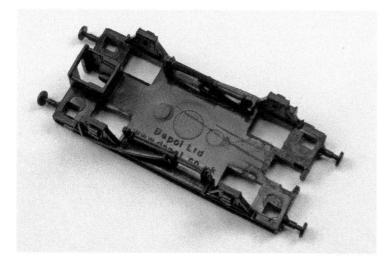

The destructive part of the process is now to remove the coupler pockets. A chassis such as this can be made from quite a hard plastic for strength and to prevent wear in the cups that hold the pinpoint ends of the axles, yet it can still be fragile and flexible. Therefore, care is needed when cutting off the pockets, as well as a sharp craft knife.

You can buy Micro-Trains couplers pre-assembled, though they are expensive, which could be a consideration if you wish to fit them to a lot of rolling stock. A cheaper alternative is to buy the couplers in kit form to make up yourself. Each one has six parts ranging from small to tiny, as comparison with the adjacent coin shows. The first few might take you an hour to put together, but like all production lines, you will soon speed up with practice.

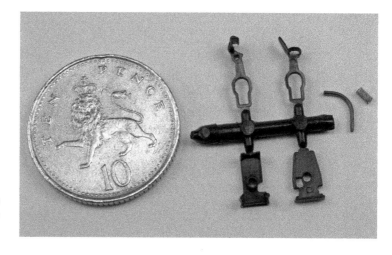

You can simply glue a Micro-Trains coupler to the chassis, though as can be seen from the assembled example on the left, there are openings in the top of the casing and sides, which make it difficult to protect the inner workings from the ingress of excess glue. The coupler kits come with a small screw that fits through the coupler. For ease of fixing, a piece of plastic card has been glued to the top of the chassis into which a 1mm hole has been drilled to accept the screw.

The driving reason for fitting Micro-Trains couplers is the ability to perform hands-off uncoupling and this is achieved by using magnets. This does mean that any other magnetic materials in the wagon must be removed, usually just the balance weight. If metal wheels are fitted, replace them with plastic ones or non-ferrous ones, such as those used on this Dapol chassis. The Micro-Trains coupler works best with heavier models, so it is necessary to replace the balance weight, in this case with some self-adhesive lead strip.

A difficulty when fitting Micro-Trains couplers to a variety of different chassis is to get them all at the same height, although they will still operate with up to 1mm variance in height. To help overcome this problem, Micro-Trains sell a gauge that sits on a piece of track and is an effective tool to check that all couplers are at the same correct height.

The position of the trip pins is critical to the operation of the system. Micro-Trains sell a useful guide tool to make sure that they are all installed on vehicles at the correct height. Sometimes the pins need adjustment to get them to respond correctly. The unique magnetic field to pull trip pins in opposing directions requires quite a large magnet to be buried under the layout, and it needs to be as close to the surface as possible for the magnetic field to work.

Finally, it is a magnetically actuated system, but anything else that's ferrous can cause problems. Most British models have a piece of steel in them to give the model some ballast weight. These weights can interfere with the correct operation of the magnet and are best replaced with some non-ferrous ballast, such as brass or lead. This often means some level of disassembly of the vehicle to effect the conversion. Some of the smaller British wagons just don't have enough bulk to operate the knuckle couplers correctly.

One final advantage to the Micro-Trains coupler is that on many vehicles, it actually looks real. A lot of rolling stock, particularly modern vehicles, actually use knuckle couplers. Although the Micro-Trains coupler is still vastly over-scale by comparison, it looks a lot more realistic than a Rapido coupler.

DAPOL KNUCKLE COUPLER

As the patents have now expired on the Micro-Trains coupler, most of the other major manufacturers can be expected to introduce their own version of the working delayed-action uncoupler. First to market is Dapol. Unlike the Micro-Trains coupler, these couplers will fit into the NEM pockets on British models.

HOOK AND LATCH COUPLERS

This covers a range of similar couplers from a number of cottage industry suppliers, such as DG Couplings, B&B and MBM. The basic design has been around for over twenty years. One of its main attractions is that, like the Micro-Trains coupler, it is a delayed-action coupler. After uncoupling over a permanent magnet or electromagnet, a wagon can be propelled to wherever it needs to be.

Also like the Micro-Trains coupler, installation is a destructive process with the complete removal of the existing coupler. None of the versions of the hook and latch coupler are available ready-made; they all have to be put together. Components need to be separated from a brass etch, and some folding and soldering is required. They can be quite temperamental to get to work and can need regular adjustment to ensure

Dapol have introduced a sprung knuckle-coupler similar to the Micro-Trains type; however, Dapol's coupler will fit directly into the NEM pocket, as usually found on the new generation of N gauge models.

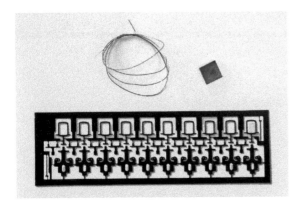

Hook and latch couplers need to be assembled and fitted to rolling stock (permanently replacing the factory-fitted couplers). As with these B&B couplers, they come on an etched fret and need to be constructed by folding and soldering. Small square magnets placed under the track allow hands-off and delayed action uncoupling.

effective operation. They are fairly discreet in terms of size, although the colour of brass is hard to hide. Some are sold already chemically blackened, which is helpful as they cannot be painted and still work.

Some modellers build a simpler version of the hook and latch coupler by having a male and female coupling at each end. This does mean that vehicles

cannot be turned round once converted. Hook and latch couplers are not for the fainthearted but if you only have a modest collection of rolling stock, then with a little perseverance they offer a cheap but effective coupling for N gauge.

CLOSE-COUPLING MECHANISMS

One of the best developments on coaching stock (and some wagons) has been the use of close-coupling systems. The tight corners used on model railways, compared to the prototype, means that the ends of rolling stock need to be further apart than they should be to allow clearance round the curves and to prevent buffer-locking. This means that on straight track, the vehicles look too far apart. A close-coupling mechanism is sprung so that vehicles are drawn together on the straight for close coupling, but they are allowed to naturally separate on curves to the required clearance for the curve.

Used in conjunction with replacement dummy knuckle couplers in NEM pockets, this simple modern development allows vehicles so fitted to appear very close together on the straight, while passing around tight curves without fear of derailing.

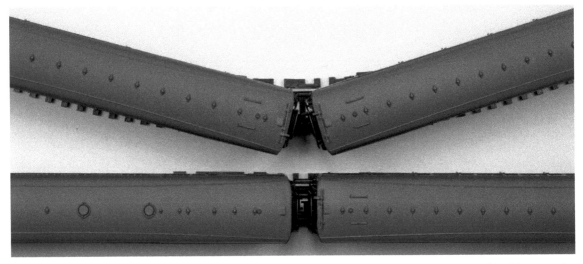

The first coaches to feature a close-coupling mechanism were Dapol's Gresley coaches, as used in this example. Even with Rapido couplings fitted, on the straight they are quite close together, while on a 9in (229mm) curve, as shown here, the coaches flex apart to accommodate the curve while remaining coupled together.

CHAPTER NINE

RAILWAY INFRASTRUCTURE

The scenery that nestles with the track itself is the railway infrastructure; it consists of all the paraphernalia that a real railway needs to operate efficiently and safely – signals and signal boxes, bridges, tunnels, station platforms and level crossings. The railway infrastructure beyond the track is a scenic element; it is part of the setting for the railway. Railway infrastructure is also the bridging element between the track, turnouts and trains, and the broader scenic setting (rural or urban). Some elements, such as signal boxes, are scenic elements that are very much part of the track. Others, such as level crossings and tunnels, are an interface between the railway and the scenery itself.

Railways need a surprising amount of infrastructure for safe and efficient operation. Some of this infrastructure is necessary to literally support the railway, such as bridges and viaducts. Other infrastructure helps the railway interact with its surroundings such as tunnels and level crossings. Further types of infrastructure are necessary for operation, such as platforms for people and signals for control.

A simple N gauge model railway that is just a single track wending its way through some fields requires no railway infrastructure. Yet as railway modellers, we're not just interested in the trains. A few bridges (either over or under the railway or both) and at least one station add in a bit more interest, as well as some operational variety. Some scenic features may be forced upon us – a tunnel to disguise an entrance to a fiddle yard is an ever-popular but ever-practical device. Some may be used to break up a scene, such as a road over-bridge. The rest are a matter of personal taste and choice.

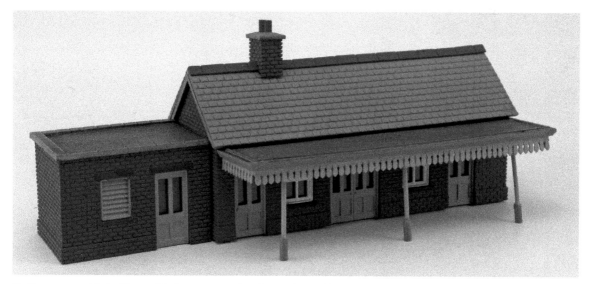

Railways were big builders of infrastructure for the track itself and for the customer. Most N gauge layouts will feature at least one station, so you will need platforms and some kind of station building. This example has been made from a Peco kit and represents a modest-sized country station that would be suitable for most eras and locations.

TUNNELS

The builders of real railways tried to avoid tunnels, as they are a costly construction enterprise; yet railway modellers love them, as there is nothing quite so obviously railway-related as a train entering or exiting a tunnel. Practically, they are a classic stage exit to the fiddle yard. Yet tunnels still need to be constructed with caution; most tunnel portals are taller than the height of a bridge. When there is no train moving through it, a tunnel may just look like a large hole in the back scene that separates the layout from the fiddle yard. Real tunnels are dark and gloomy affairs. A tunnel mouth that is part of the back scene does not look realistic because the fiddle yard can be seen through it.

The majority of real tunnels start in a cutting. Modelling this approach and some of the land over the tunnel mouth creates a more realistic imitation of the train disappearing into a long tunnel, rather than a fiddle yard. Another way to hide a fiddle yard is literally

with 'tunnel vision', modelling the first few inches of the internal tunnel wall, preferably painted black.

There are plenty of commercially produced tunnel mouths available in N gauge, which understandably reflects the popularity of tunnels as a practical scenic feature. Peco have produced their single- and double-track portals for many years. These are very popular and understandably so. They are moulded in lightweight plastic, which can be painted to represent whatever 'local' stone is appropriate for the part of the country you are modelling. They also include a set of retaining wall 'wings' for either side of the portal. The inner ring of the tunnel mouth has a slot to accept an inner tunnel wall made from cardboard to represent the beginnings of the bore.

A number of 'cottage industry' manufacturers make tunnel portals cast in plaster. These are good products, easily painted, though if weight is an issue for a portable layout, they may add a little to the overall heaviness. There's an even greater

A tunnel is a classic feature for a model railway, even if engineers avoided them in real life. This is a plastic double-track tunnel portal from Peco, which has been painted and weathered. Note how the tunnel lining has been included so that the inside looks dark, like a real tunnel, and the fiddle yard on the other side cannot be seen.

range of tunnel portals if you look to Continental and American products. In many respects, a tunnel portal does the same job wherever it is in the world, so many of these are suitable for a British setting. Even if some of these seem overly fancy, with crenellation and castellation, there are a surprising number of real tunnel portals in Britain with more than a pinch of the 'fairy tale castle' about them. They are often seemingly in the middle of nowhere but they were made this way to appease the local landowner when the railways first arrived.

BRIDGES

Railway bridges over or under things are far more commonplace in real life than tunnels. Each bridge on a line has a sequential number and it is surprising how high the number can be just a short distance away from one end of the line. Unlike tunnels, bridges come in all shapes and sizes from small affairs over streams to huge constructions like viaducts. Fortunately, there is a good range of products in N gauge to bridge the gap.

Some products are only suitable as road overbridges. Peco's dependable plastic bridge kits for either single- or double-track stone bridges are one example. Like the tunnel portals, they come with retaining 'wings' but without a deck. This is left to the builder, so that the required width of the bridge can be customized, which is easy to do with a piece of card that fits into the moulded slot inside the bridge.

Bridges are very useful scenic features and you can take full advantage of this in N gauge. They can add height to an otherwise flat scene, break up a layout into scenic sections, or hide the entrance to a fiddle yard. This scratch-built road bridge on Glazebrook by the Warrington Model Railway club makes a nice scene next to the elevated signal box, while the similar bridges in the background hide the entrance to the fiddle yard.

Staying with stone bridges, Ratio produce a viaduct 'system' of stone arches made in plastic. These can be built as a low bridge, such as would cross a river, or, with the addition of pillars, the bridge can be turned into a viaduct. Multiple kits can be joined together to make a viaduct as long as you require, to take advantage of the huge scenic possibilities of N gauge.

Long bridges carrying the railway on a curve are best avoided, as they can present problems with the sharp curves that are typical on model railways. Short bridges on curves are possible as, with most bridge kits, the deck can be made wide enough to allow sufficient clearance for coaches overhanging in the middle. Bridges that cross curved track or cross straight track at an acute angle are also easy to do as the bridge deck can be made as long as required to give clearance to the railway lines underneath.

Arched bridges representing stone or brick construction can have limited clearance for track, such that they are only suitable for straight track passing under at a right-angle. More flexible are girder bridges between abutments. Peco make a set of bridge girders that will span a double track at an angle or on a curve. Successive sets of these girders can be joined with intermediate supporting pillars to make a longer bridge or viaduct.

If the Peco bridge girders are too short, or even too long for the gap you want to bridge, you can easily scratch build your own bridge girders from plastic sheet detailed with plastic strip (alternatively, simply use cardboard). Whatever girders you use, you will still have to build the abutments, but these are usually simple brick affairs with square edges, which are easy to achieve by wrapping brick paper or plastic brick sheet around a suitably sized block of wood. Peco do a set of truss-girder sides (a trapezoid shape angled at each end) that can be used 'over girder' (where the trains run 'through' the bridge') or 'under girder' (where the trains run over the bridge).

As with tunnels, it's worth looking to Continental and American producers for bridges, especially if you want something a bit more substantial. The Warren Truss bridge (like the Peco product) was a popular all-steel construction in the United States, and so models are widely available. There were some substantial girder bridges on the Continent, especially over rivers and in mountains, models for which are available.

Finally, bridges are not something that are necessarily scale-specific. If you cannot find the N gauge bridge you are looking for, try the larger scales (mainly OO gauge). For example, a small, single-track girder bridge for OO gauge may be just right as a large, double-track bridge in N gauge.

STATION PLATFORMS

It's likely that your N gauge model railway will have at least one station, so you will need to have platforms for your passengers. Station platforms are a standard height, although the width can vary, and of course the length, from a small rural halt to a big city terminus. Therefore, the thing to look for in commercially available platform systems for N gauge is their flexibility in terms of width and length.

You can make your own platforms quite easily, using just a piece of wood of the right thickness to represent the correct height. This can be faced with plastic or paper brick sheet, and plastic or paper sheet for the platform surface, be it flags or macadam. Remember that if you have used a cork or foam underlay, you will have to raise the platform slightly to compensate for the thickness of the underlay.

Real platform sides have a little relief at the top, especially the older brick-built ones. A good representation of this can be to use the Peco plastic platform edging – this is available to represent brick, stone or concrete sides, and the corresponding ramps at the platform ends as well. You have to provide your own platform surface, but it is a flexible and easily extended system, especially if you want to model bay platforms. Peco also make complete platform kits that include the top surface (which can be trimmed to one of three predetermined widths). They also produce a set of subway steps to fit in the middle of a platform, for stations where passengers cross the line by means of a subway rather than a bridge. Platform models are also available from Metcalfe models in card, and Ratio and Kestrel in plastic. The latter manufacturers also make platform canopy kits.

The main consideration when installing platforms is to ensure that there is adequate clearance for rolling stock. This is particularly important in N gauge, since the smaller scale means that tolerances for the gap between the platform edge and trains are smaller. Start by drawing a line, using a classic technique for measuring clearances. Hold a pencil in the middle of a coach and then run it up and down a few times to leave a line.

Place the base of the platform edging (in this case, the plastic Peco edging) against the line and test for clearance. The edges of real platforms are built out at the top and most model products will reflect this; therefore, clearance is initially very realistic but actually too tight to be workable.

Ease the base of the platform edging back from the drawn line until the gap allows sufficient clearance for rolling stock without looking overly unrealistic. Try the widest piece of rolling stock that will be used on the layout, particularly steam locomotives with outside cylinders, such as this Dapol Prairie tank. Some models can actually be wider than they should be over the cylinders to allow clearance for bogie wheels between them. Once you are satisfied that the gap is correct, mark the baseboard at the back of the platform edging.

Measure the line made at the back of the platform edging (in this case, 14mm). The measurement has been taken from the edge of the rail; while the sleepers should be straight, if the track has been laid correctly, then you are guaranteed that the rail is straight. Mark 14mm from the rail along the length of where the platform will be and then join the marks with a ruler, so that you have a straight line. This line is a guide to work to when gluing the platform edges to the baseboard.

You may find it easier to work on the platforms away from the layout. As an alternative to gluing the platform edging directly to the baseboard, cut a strip of plastic card to the width of the lines drawn in the previous step. The platform edging can then be glued to the strip of plastic. Note the two track pins (with heads removed) near the end of the left-hand piece of platform edging – these serve as a guide to relocate the platform in exactly the right place, whenever it is removed from the layout.

If you need to shorten the Peco plastic platform edging pieces or go around a corner, then use a razor saw in a mitre block to ensure accurate cuts. Platform edging actually leans inwards slightly towards the platform, so hold the edging piece upright when cutting 45-degree mitres, as here.

RIGHT: Once all the platform edges are in place, you need to add a surface between them. This photograph shows (from left to right) the three stages involved. First, add some supports between the platform edges; this is particularly important for very wide platforms. In this case, the supports are the height of the inner edge of the Peco platform edging. Second, add sheets of card or plastic card to cover the platform to a depth that is just below the outer edge. Third, add the platform surface, in this case, grey plastic flag effect from Slaters. The plastic top layer is about ¹⁄₃₂in (0.5mm) thick, whereas a printed paper effect layer would be much thinner. Therefore, it is important to test the middle and top layers together to make sure that when combined, they will be flush with the edge.

BELOW: It is much easier in N gauge to add the final platform details, such as lamps, luggage and fencing, while the platform model is off the layout. Once this work is done, the completed platform (now with station building) can be permanently installed on the layout. Then the ballasting and scenic work can be finished around the platform, as with this view of Tunley Marsh.

Keep platforms to the straight track and avoid all but the most generous of curves. As coaches overhang in the middle while traversing a curve, you need to allow generous clearances for the platforms – the sharper the curve, the bigger the unrealistic gaps between the platform and the coach ends. It is also quite difficult to accurately curve the platform itself, and plastic components, such as the Peco system, will be difficult to bend.

LEVEL CROSSINGS

If you don't fancy a bridge to take a road over or under the railway tracks, you can keep things on the level. Real railways had, and still have, thousands of level crossings, although they didn't like them, as they not only had to be maintained, they also had to be staffed (unless they came under the control of a signal box).

Level crossing gates are easy to add to an N gauge layout, since a number of kits are available, such as this one from Peco. The hard part is laying a road surface across the rails that will not interfere with rolling stock as it passes. This example has the added complexity of being built on a curve, yet the long wheelbase of the Class 9F locomotive will easily pass over it.

One of the challenges for modelling a level-crossing is to get the road surface to cross the rails without interfering with the rolling stock's wheels or catching the bottom of a locomotive mechanism or a coupler pin. The road surface needs to be set just below rail height, and the part of the crossing that goes between the rails must allow enough clearance for the wheel flanges.

Steam-era crossing gates and the modern-era lifting barriers are available from Peco. If you are concerned about being able to build your own level crossing, Peco include one in their sectional track range; this can be easily joined to flexible track, if that is what you are using. The Peco level crossing can cleverly be extended to include as many parallel tracks as required. The road approach is pretty steep on these crossings but it is easily integrated into a scenic road.

White metal kits are available from Langley Models and P&D Marsh, while Kestrel produces a very nice crossing-keeper's cottage that comes with a simple set of gates.

SIGNALS AND SIGNAL BOXES

Signalling is another thing that makes your layout look like a railway, although to many modellers, it's another one of those incomprehensible black arts. So much so, that a lot of modellers simply omit signals altogether, even though they may include a signal box. Signals are traffic lights for trains and are found where trains need to be controlled to avoid accidents. A simple station halt will not need any signals, but as soon as you introduce junctions and passing loops, you need signals for control.

Signals themselves come in an unbelievable variety.

There is a basic distinction between semaphore signals (the moving arm on a post) and coloured light signals. All of the steam-era railway companies had their own style of semaphore signals – concrete, lattice or wooden posts, upper or lower quadrant (a level arm always means 'danger' or 'stop' but the 'clear' position could be represented by the arm moving up or down, thus describing the quadrant). Although the components were the same, most signals were a bespoke build for a specific location, depending on sighting, whether a junction or even when a signal gantry was needed to support many signals. Coloured-light signals are a little more uniform in their design, though there are two-aspect (red and green), three-aspect (red, yellow and green) and even four-aspect (red, single yellow, double yellow and green) types.

Most N gauge semaphore signals are available as kits, either for a single signal or a bracket signal. The finest examples are the plastic kits from Ratio, which can even be made to work, although they are difficult for the beginner to construct. Slightly more robust are the ranges in white metal from P&D Marsh and Langley Models. Each manufacturer's kits can be adapted to make more complex signals, such as double bracket signals or gantries.

A challenge for model semaphore signals in any scale is to make them work; in N gauge this is an even greater challenge. Non-working signals will display the same aspect all the time, so you either have to pass the signal at danger (Signal Passed At Danger, known as 'SPAD') or have all the signals 'clear' all the time. Therefore, the recently introduced range of signals from Dapol is most welcome. Not only are they ready-made, so that there is none of the difficulty of making such a fragile model, the arm operates and there is even a Light Emitting Diode to illuminate the red or green lens on the signal arm. The signals simply secure into a hole drilled into the baseboard with just four wires for the operation.

Working coloured-light signals have always been easier to manufacture, since there are no moving parts, only light bulbs. Berko make a wide range of signals with two- and three-colour aspects. These signals are easily fixed to a layout with just a few wires for their operation.

This is a single-post, single-arm starter or home signal produced as a plastic kit by Ratio. It can be further detailed by the purchase of separate brass detailing parts from Ratio, such as the access ladder. It can also be made to work, though this can be a bit tricky.

Signals need a signal box to control them. Signal boxes come in as much variety as the signals they control; once again a result of circumstance and the aesthetic architectural styling of individual railway companies. There are several good plastic kits, from Ratio, Peco and Kestrel, as well as card kits from Metcalfe. Some, like the Ratio GWR signal box, are very particular to a railway company, while others represent the more generic brick and wood constructions found all over the UK. Most of these kits are easy to make, but if you're unsure, there are ready-made versions in the Hornby Lyddle End and Bachmann Scenecraft ranges. These only tend to be made in small batches so they are not always available.

Dapol have introduced the first working semaphore signals in N gauge. They simply require a hole to be drilled into the baseboard to accept the motor housing underneath, which is then held in place by a plastic nut that screws on to the thread on the motor housing.

Once the Dapol signal has been fixed in place, ballast can be glued to the base and surroundings. Take care not to get glue or ballast into the hole for the operating linkage. Four wires underneath provide power and control via a simple push button. A Light Emitting Diode illuminates the 'lamp' so that the correct red or green aspect shows as the semaphore arm moves.

MOTIVE POWER DEPOTS

A steam- or diesel-era motive power depot always makes an interesting feature on any N gauge layout, or even makes a layout in itself. Locomotive servicing and maintenance has always required substantial and specialized railway infrastructure, such as turntables. The popularity of the subject has attracted the attention of the manufacturers, so these scenes can be readily represented in N gauge.

Locomotive sheds can be big or small, so both Peco and Ratio make building kits that can be made as a small single-road facility for a branch line, or joined together in multiples, as many times as necessary, to make much bigger installations. Peco make versions for both the steam era and the modern era. Metcalfe make a very good card kit that can be similarly joined in multiples. Hornby Lyddle End and Bachmann Scenecraft have ready-made models of small and large sheds. Another signature feature of sheds and depots is the

LEFT: Coloured-light signals, appropriate to the modernized railway from the 1950s onwards, are produced by a number of manufacturers, such as this one by Berko. It represents a three-light (red, yellow, green) single signal and is fully working by simply connecting the signal's wires to an appropriate three-way switch.

BELOW: Peco's signal box kit is a nice generic design suitable for most layouts (based on a real Saxby and Farmer pre-grouping design). It's a simple plastic kit with good instructions, which makes an excellent starting point for anyone new to plastic-building construction.

structions for major towns and cities to the more typical single through-road versions of small country stations.

Peco and Ratio make plastic kits for goods sheds while Metcalfe make a cardboard kit. P&D Marsh sell a very detailed and accurate model of the shed at Watlington, which is made from a mix of laser-cut plywood and white-metal parts. Like locomotive sheds, most of these kits can be joined in multiples to make a more extensive structure.

ELECTRIFIED LINES

Electric power for railways is not a new invention, but since World War Two it has become much more widespread on both suburban lines and main lines. There are two basic systems to supply the electric

maintenance pits that run between the rails; these are available as a kit from Peco and simply fit into a slot in the baseboard and join to their existing track range.

Other railway buildings, such as water towers and coaling stages for steam trains, and fuelling points and tanks for diesels, are available in kit or ready-made form. For large steam-era depots, Peco make a turntable kit that can be motorized.

GOODS SHEDS

A goods shed is a mainly steam-era piece of infrastructure, with most out of use by the late 1960s, thanks to modernization and containerization. It is the classic goods yard building from massive warehouse-like con-

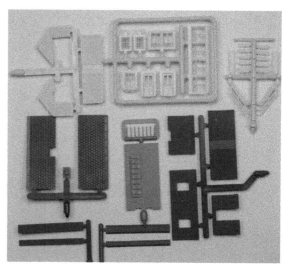

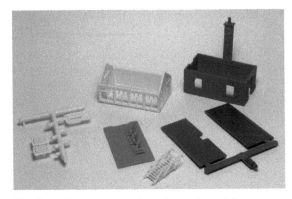

The Peco kit uses pre-coloured plastic, so it's not necessary to paint it; however, even coloured plastic can still look like plastic, so a coat of paint will improve the finish enormously. In order to make it easier to paint the different sections in different colours, the model has been constructed as a series of sub-assemblies, while some of the smaller parts, such as the door and windows for the lower storey, have been left on the sprue for ease of handling.

power to a moving train – a ground-level third rail, or a suspended wire (catenary) above the train.

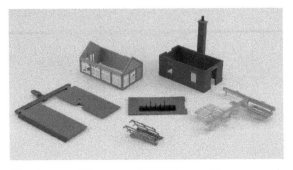

All sub-assemblies were given a spray with an aerosol primer (there are specific plastic compatible ones, but the types sold for car body repairs work just as well). Some signal-box paint schemes were quite complex, such as the upper storey for this GWR version, which features 'light stone', 'dark stone' and white window frames.

THIRD RAIL

There are no commercially available components in N gauge for adding a third rail to your layout; however, it can still be modelled without too much difficulty. Prototype third-rail systems usually have the

All the individual components have now been united to produce the finished model of the signal box. The windows have been glazed internally with the clear plastic sheet supplied with the kit.

This model of a GWR timber-frame signal-box is produced by Ratio as a plastic kit with some etched-brass details, such as the window frames.

rail on the outside edge of the track, supported on insulators. The ceramic insulators are quite small so there's no real need to represent them in N gauge. Their supporting job can be carried out by track pins, which can be inserted into pre-drilled holes on the outer edge of sleepers. The trick is to get all the pins at the same height – a simple guide to stop the pins being driven in too far is all that is required.

The third rail itself can be represented with rail from track; simply slide the sleepers off. One yard (metre) of flexible track will provide two yards (two metres) of third rail. Try to find rail with the lowest profile, at least Code 55, to avoid it looking over-scale. As a final touch, use plastic strip to represent the wooden guard on the outside that is there to protect staff in depots and stations. Now that there is at least one ready-to-run third-rail EMU model in N gauge, there's every reason for considering a third-rail-equipped layout.

This single-road engine shed from Peco is typical of the plastic kit offerings from a number of manufacturers. It will accommodate all but the largest steam locomotives; however, like most of the other kits, it can be joined to additional kits, both widthways and lengthways, to make a shed as large as you require.

OVERHEAD ELECTRIFICATION

Overhead electrification, otherwise called catenary, is a more commercially supported prospect in N gauge. Prototype railways support the wire using either single posts with a bracketed arm or a gantry across numerous tracks.

It is first of all worth a look at Continental-manufactured systems; Continental railways have long

Most goods yards in the steam era had a goods shed of some sort. Size and type of construction varied enormously but there are several kits for modest-sized stations available in N gauge. The plastic kit from Ratio for a single-road goods shed is full of superb detail for N gauge and careful construction and painting will result in an outstanding model that will not take up too much space.

This goods shed kit, manufactured by P&D Marsh, is a replica of the goods shed at Watlington. The kit is made from neither card nor plastic, as you might expect; instead it consists of a series of sheets of very thin plywood that have been laser-cut to produce the required shapes. This is a very common method of kit manufacture in America and it is becoming increasingly common in N gauge in Britain.

made extensive use of overhead electrification, so it is well supported by manufacturers. To the expert eye, there are a lot of differences between the construction of the prototype Continental systems and British systems; however, if you are happy to accept that it's all just posts and gantries, then there are some good models to be found, such as those produced by Volmer. For the serious British modeller, Dapol have recently introduced a single mast catenary, which is a faithful reproduction of the British type.

The biggest question for modellers of catenary in N gauge is whether or not to actually model the wire. In fact, catenary wire is not just one wire

strung between two poles like telephone wires. It is actually a wire hung from a wire for reasons of strength and electrical isolation from the supporting structure. Because of this, real catenary can look like a mass of knitting. In real life, the cable is quite thin, such that once it is scaled down to N gauge, it would be extremely thin. Some modellers feel that it's not worth modelling the wire itself as the supporting infrastructure of masts and gantries provides enough visual representation. Certainly, unless you use a complete commercial system, you could find that fitting the wire is a fiddly process, especially on a large layout.

This is a British prototype single-mast overhead wire-support from Dapol. It simply requires a hole to be drilled into the baseboard top for the mast, which is secured underneath with a plastic wing nut. They come inexpensively in packs of ten so that it does not cost too much to build a long electrified mainline.

Catenary can be fragile stuff in real life – severe winds can cause damage and disruption. While the modeller does not face the perils of the weather, big fingers can do as much damage to the model, if, say, trying to recover a derailed wagon. This is another reason, perhaps, for not going the whole way with catenary. Even cleaning the track could be difficult.

The pantograph (the metal wiper on an electric locomotive's roof that draws power from overhead cables) on most model locomotives is usually sprung and can be set to stay at a certain height. While on very close inspection, the pantograph may actually be wiping nothing more than thin air, from a normal viewing distance, and at even moderate speed, it should look sufficiently realistic. Even with the wire in place, unless the pantograph is sprung such that it maintains contact with the wire, it will be very difficult to set the pantograph height so that it stays in contact with the wire all the time.

Most of the major electric locomotive classes from the last fifty years are now available ready-to-run in N gauge, as well as a few EMUs. Overhead electrification is a fascinating type of railway, and it is well supported in N gauge.

WHITE METAL KITS

There are many kits in N gauge for both railway and non-railway items that are made from white metal, so it is worth looking at how to make them. No special skills are required, but it is useful to know how to work with white metal, simply because there is such a vast array of detail items available. No model railway

Modelling overhead electrification (known as catenary) can be a challenge in any scale, not least N gauge. The results can be stunning, as with this scene on Kinlet Wharf by the Wye Forrest Model Railway Club, where not only the gantries but also the wires have all been faithfully modelled.

in N gauge can afford to be without a selection of items made from white metal.

White metal is a relatively soft alloy made from lead and tin. Note the lead part of the composition – it is perfectly safe to work with, but do remember to wash your hands after handling. It is easy to cast quite small and intricate shapes and details, so it is ideal for even the smallest items in N gauge. When cast thinly, it is soft enough that it can be bent (intentionally or otherwise), so hold any potentially fragile items with care.

The hardest part with white metal is cleaning the castings, since the moulds used often produce a lot of 'flash' (this is the leakage from the joint between the two parts of the mould). Use an old 'rat tail' file to file away the excess metal. Old or very cheap files are recommended because the soft metal will soon clog the teeth of a file that is designed for use on harder metals, such as brass. Time and care spent at this stage will ensure that the finished item looks neat and tidy, as well as ensuring a good fit for the various parts.

White metal kits usually only consist of a few parts and they can be easily joined together with superglue or a two-part epoxy glue. There is no need to solder the parts together (with a special low melting point solder), although you can if you have the necessary skills; indeed, such simple kits make an excellent introduction to learning this skill. The completed model should be cleaned with a glass-fibre burnishing brush to remove any tarnishing and then it is advisable to paint it with a primer (cheap aerosol primers for car body repairs are ideal). After that, it can be painted as you would any other model.

Many white metal details are small enough to be single items, such as benches for platforms, so they just need to be cleaned and painted. Be aware that the quality of white metal castings can vary from the perfect to the less than perfect, although even the latter can usually be cleaned and bent into a reasonable representation of what they are supposed to be. The major producers of white metal kits in N gauge, such as Langley Models and P&D Marsh, have a solid reputation for quality items. So check out the extensive ranges from these and other producers in order to add a host of fine details to your N gauge model railway.

Once constructed, white metal kits need to be cleaned with a glass-fibre burnishing brush and then primed with a car aerosol primer to give a good base for top coats that are resistant to chipping and scratching. This is a finished P&D Marsh kit for a GWR water crane (complete with 'fire devil' heater to stop the water freezing in winter) that will add a superb detail to an N gauge layout.

N gauge modellers are spoilt for choice in terms of the detail kits that are available in white metal for both railway and non-railway related items. It is an easy material to work with and the kits need nothing more sophisticated than superglue to put together. This is a selection of railway infrastructure: a loading gauge and a platform-mounted water crane from P&D Marsh, and a three-ton yard crane from Springside Models.

CHAPTER TEN

SCENERY AND BUILDINGS

You may be quite happy to just clip some sectional track together on the dining table and watch a train going round and round. Yet it is likely that you will want to frame the train in a realistic setting. The first step is to build a baseboard as a foundation for the track, but it is also a foundation for the surrounding scenery.

Beyond the railway infrastructure of stations and tunnels lies the real scenery, the setting that defines your layout, be it urban, rural, coastal or a combination of one or more scenes. Urban scenery needs streets, houses, factories and shops. Rural scenery needs hills, streams, farms and trees. All of this can be done very effectively in N gauge, where its space-saving properties mean that you can have epic scenic vistas in quite a modest amount of space. While the design of a track plan might be considered to be engineering in miniature, filling in around it with scenery is like painting a picture.

URBAN LANDSCAPE

Most major stations and rail centres are situated in towns and cities. The large populations to be found there mean that there are lots of passengers and

Card kits are a simple and cost-effective way of rapidly developing urban scenery (or any requirement for buildings). The extensive range from Metcalfe is extremely popular with modellers in N gauge. Only a few simple tools are needed, as shown here, and a suitable card or paper glue. Pre-printed windows on acetate are included, while everything else is pre-coloured on the main sheet. The coloured pencils are for finishing any white edges of the card that may be visible on the finished model.

freight. If you want to model a sizable station, the surrounding landscape needs to be urban. There might be the odd municipal park with some grass to break things up, but basically you need lots of streets and lots of buildings. The space-saving properties of N gauge mean that you can really go to town with your town planning.

You will need lots of buildings: some may need to be different, such as warehouses and factories, while some may need to be repeated, such as rows of terraced houses. Fortunately, there are lots of urban buildings available in N gauge as kits from Metcalfe and Kestrel, and as ready-made from Hornby Lyddle End and Bachmann Scenecraft. Many of these buildings are easily modified, either to fit a specific location or to inject a little variety.

Buildings placed at the very back of the layout, against the back scene, can be modelled in low relief. With kits, this means that you can use the front half of a building in one place and the back half in another.

A lot of the urban landscape is just roofs. If the front or rear of a building faces to the back of the layout, it may never be seen from any of the normal viewing positions. In that case, it is not necessary to finish that side of the model in any great detail, as it will never be seen. This speeds things up a bit. Building a large urban

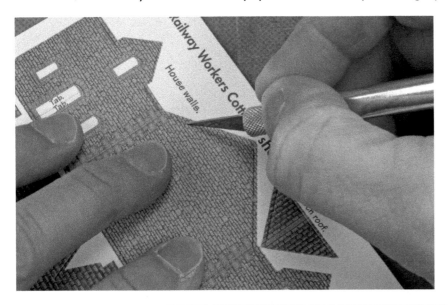

The first task is to remove the parts from the main sheet. This is very straightforward because they are die-cut all the way through, apart from a number of small tabs that are easy to cut with a sharp knife.

Window openings are die-cut all the way around – simply 'pop' the waste material out with the tip of a knife. The material in the doorway is clearly marked 'tab'. This must not be removed, and it folds inwards to add depth to the door opening.

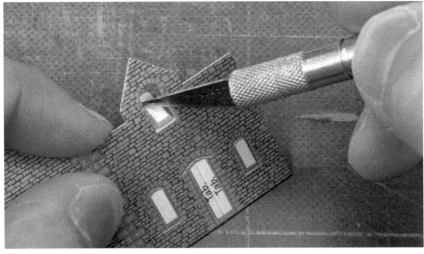

The window glazing is cut from the acetate sheet and glued behind the window openings. Use the fine applicator nozzle on the card glue to add the barest amount of glue around the window. Then use tweezers to place the glazing behind the window, checking from the front that it is aligned correctly.

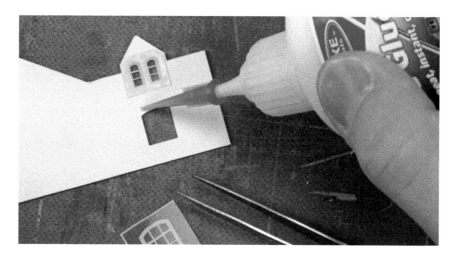

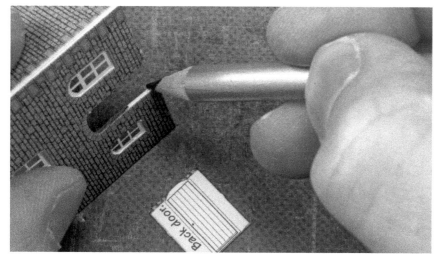

Where the tabs have been folded back for the doorways, the white edge of the card will show. This can be coloured by painting or, as here, simply coloured in with a black pencil.

The walls of the building are glued around an inner former. This is where the ease of construction with these kits is most obvious, since there is no need to worry about getting the corners straight – it's been done for you. The shell of the building quickly attains a structural integrity that will withstand subsequent handling.

The main roof is a single piece that has been pre-scored down the ridge line. It only needs to be flexed slightly to open up the score line a little and then it can be glued to the building. Pre-cut paper ridge tiles are included in the kit and they cover the white edges of the card, which would otherwise be visible on the ridge line.

Barge boards, chimneys, even chimney pots are included in the kits and these provide some of those essential finishing touches that add detail to the model. You can add your own extra details, such as gutters and drainpipes, which can be made from pieces of wire.

The completed Metcalfe building looks really effective and would suit any N gauge layout. The fact that it is assembled in a few hours and costs just a few pounds means that you can quickly develop a large urban scene.

Low-relief buildings can be placed at the rear of a layout to form part of the back scene. Only the front of the building needs to be modelled and often you can cut a building down the middle and get two for the price of one. Here is another of the excellent Metcalfe card building kits for N gauge – this one is actually designed as just the front of the building for a low-relief effect.

Hedges Hill Cutting by Grahame Hedges was one of the first N gauge layouts to really portray the idea of a railway as part of an urban landscape nestling alongside factories, houses and shops. Virtually everything in this scene has been scratch built, while the third-rail EMUs were built from kits. Photo: Grahame Hedges

landscape means filling it with models, whereas making a large rural landscape can be accomplished more quickly if it is mainly fields with a few trees.

All the buildings will need to be linked by streets and roads. These can simply be painted onto card and white lines added as needed (depending on location and era). There are commercially available road surfaces, mainly from Continental manufacturers, but these are perfectly suitable (as long as you remember to drive on the correct side of the road). Pavements are available from Metcalfe and Langley Models, or they can be made from thin card topped with plastic sheet or paper to represent flags.

Give some consideration as to how the railway will sit in the urban landscape that you are creating. If you keep everything on the flat, in other words, the buildings and track are on the same level, there is a risk that the trains will get lost in the 'urban jungle'. Even a terraced house is quite tall next to railway rolling stock, never mind a much higher building such as a factory or warehouse.

Real railways are built on the level as much as possible, even though the land around them rises and falls. Many urban railways have had to be built over the existing townscape. There are many miles of railway built on arches in an urban environment. It's worth, therefore, elevating the railway above ground level so that it is less dominated by the surrounding scenery – after all, you want to be able to see your model trains most of the time.

It is hard to imagine a more convincing urban street scene than this one created by Grahame Hedges on his Stoney Lane Depot layout. There is so much detail to take in but particular note should be given to the road markings and traffic lights for the pedestrian-crossing. The road in the background is actually painted on to the back scene but it convincingly appears to disappear into the distance. Photo: Grahame Hedges

RURAL LANDSCAPE

Between the population centres of urban landscape lies an awful lot of rural landscape. The geology and flora can define a place, just as much as the style of the signal box or the train that is passing through. N gauge offers the space to develop some grand scenic views, so that you have a landscape with a railway in it, rather than a railway with a bit of landscape on it.

Unless you are modelling somewhere that is renowned for its flatness, you are going to need to introduce some hills. If you are using an open-frame baseboard, you can sit the railway on the side of a hill. More common, and much simpler, is to build the hills up from a level baseboard top. Hills require bulk and there are a number of ways to do this.

FOUNDATIONS FOR HILLS

A quick though quite messy approach is to use polystyrene sheets or polystyrene packaging. While it provides bulk without much weight, it is awfully messy stuff when you come to saw it, carve it and shape it to form the contours for hills. The electrostatic properties of those little polystyrene balls mean that they will be stuck to everything for weeks afterwards. More seriously, polystyrene can react with some ad-hesives, usually causing it to melt. It's nasty stuff in a fire, releasing all sorts of dangerous chemicals. Even the low voltages in model railways can, in very exceptional circumstances, start a fire.

A safer alternative to polystyrene is insulation foam, the type that comes in large, thick sheets for use in buildings. Not surprisingly, therefore, it already meets fire regulations. These foam materials are quite dense but they can be cut and carved to form a base for scenery with a lot less mess.

The simplest method is to make supporting contours for a scenic base. These contours can be cut from thin plywood, placed about 3in (76mm) apart. They can be cross-braced with more plywood as necessary to give strength. While scenery does not have to support any great weight, it still requires a degree of integral strength in order to survive the bumps and thumps of a portable layout, or someone accidentally leaning a hand on to it.

An alternative to plywood is to use cardboard, specifically the type of corrugated ply cardboard used in substantial packaging boxes. This is much quicker to shape than plywood, as it can be cut with just a knife, even a pair of stout scissors. It can be fixed in place with virtually all adhesives, but woodworking glue, a hot glue gun or a grab adhesive are ideal.

Only a few simple tools are needed to form scenic contours. As repeated cutting of cardboard will soon blunt a blade, use the cheap snap-off type blades and keep snapping the blade regularly to maintain a sharp cut. PVA glue is ideal for bonding card to card and card to wood, though the thicker consistency of 'grab adhesive' in a tube with a nozzle is sometimes better, as its thickness will keep pieces in place while the glue sets.

Corrugated cardboard is a lightweight material for scenery that is easily cut to shape and will take virtually any kind of glue. Best of all, it can usually be obtained for free from packaging. Several layers can be laid one on top of each other to form low-lying scenery, such as here, where three pieces have been used to build up the station forecourt area to the level of the platform.

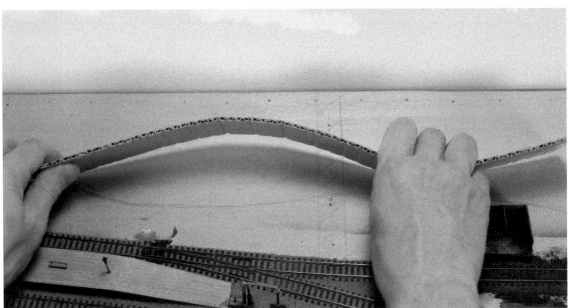

Another advantage to using corrugated cardboard is that is can be curved. First, cut a strip so that the corrugations are at a right-angle to the direction of the cut. Then gently pull the strip through your thumb and fingers at a slight angle until the corrugations crease. Turn the strip over and repeat to crease the corrugations on the other side. The strip can then be curved to any shape, even an S-shape.

This strip of corrugated cardboard is the beginning of a road at the rear of the Tunley Marsh layout, which will form a gentle S-shape, as well as rising on the right and then falling. As the road surface will twist and turn through different planes, this would be difficult to build just using formers. The first strip has been cut to length and held in place with track pins, while the incline rising from left to right has been drawn on with pencil.

The incline has now been cut out using a pair of scissors, such is the ease with which corrugated cardboard can be worked. White glue can be seen drying as this first part of the road is attached to the layout with track pins holding it in place while the glue sets.

The front edge for the road is surprisingly strong once the glue has set; however, to make it stronger and to shape the scenery in front of the road, a series of triangles of corrugated cardboard have been added at right angles to the former for the road. These are cut out with scissors and the trick is not to be too precise so as to add a little unevenness to the terrain.

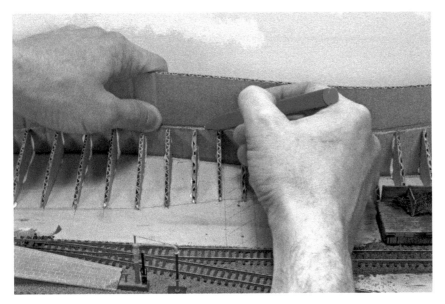

A series of additional formers can now be added for the road, one behind the other. Strips of corrugated cardboard are held behind the former for the road, which is used as a template to draw the outline of the road. The strip is then cut with scissors to the line and glued behind the former for the road. This process is repeated until the desired width of the road has been achieved.

This is an overhead view of the road after fitting twelve strips of corrugated cardboard for the road. Each has been cut to the profile of the road and then laminated together.

With the base for the road completed, the rear of the scenery can be started with more corrugated formers to define the shape. As these formers are much taller than the ones at the front, cross-pieces have been inserted between them for additional strength.

COVERING THE FOUNDATIONS

The base for the scenery needs to be something that can hold its form while the scenery is completed. Some kind of wire mesh is ideal, as it can be bent to a shape that it can hold; chicken wire is a classic source for such a material or, for small areas, the finer meshes used in car body repairs. These can be pinned or stapled to plywood formers, or glued to cardboard ones, but do be careful of sharp ends and edges where it is necessary to cut the wire or mesh.

An alternative to a metal mesh is to weave your own mesh out of thin cardboard strips. The cardboard used in cereal packets is ideal and it's free. Start by gluing or stapling strips crossways between formers, then weave in additional strips in the opposite direction. The cardboard weave can be shaped and formed, though it is not quite as precise as a metal mesh. You can give the cardboard weave a bit more shape and support by filling the gaps between the formers with lightly scrunched-up newspaper. Once the weave is complete, it is advisable to paint it with a thick coat of a white glue, such as PVA or woodworking glue, in order to bind the weave together and give it some strength.

Once the basic land form is complete, it needs a top layer adding to give a smooth coating that hides the mesh or weave underneath. If you have used a fine enough mesh or a cardboard weave, you can just trowel on a layer of plaster; this is fine for permanent layouts, but for portable layouts, the plaster may be prone to cracking over time, as the layout is moved around.

A better alternative, but still using plaster, is to use plaster-impregnated bandage, exactly as if you were setting a fracture. You can actually buy plaster-impregnated material, which is sold specifically for landscape modellers, Modroc being the most familiar brand. The material is wetted and is then pliant enough to be shaped over the mesh or weave. It dries as a hard shell, and the bandage content makes it more resistant to cracking. A cheaper alternative is to use papier mâché, sheets of newspaper bonded over the mesh or weave with wallpaper paste or PVA. Several layers may be needed to hide what's underneath, but the source material is free, with just the cost of adhesive.

Not all hilly landscapes are simply undulating grass slopes – many places feature rocky outcrops; indeed, some railway cuttings have been blasted through mountainous terrain and consist of nothing but rock. Using real rocks in small or large quantities is an option, although too many could cause weight issues. Dense foam insulating material can be made to represent certain rocky geological features, but the most common material used is plaster. Moulds are available from the likes of Woodland Scenics for you to cast your own rock faces in plaster. The resulting castings can be broken down into smaller pieces for variety and flexibility.

ADDING THE GREENERY

Once the contours of the hills are complete, it's time to start adding some greenery. The first step is to seal any porous substances, like plaster. This often requires nothing more than a coat of paint – household emulsions being ideal. Paint is best for another reason – if any of the subsequent scenic work becomes damaged or dislodged over time, you will see paint rather than glaring white plaster. For this reason, choose green or brown paint.

Grass and flowers can be represented with scatter materials. There are literally dozens of scatter materials available in a bewildering array of grass and other colours, with some very evocative names such as 'early spring meadow'. The quality and range of German company Noch and American company Woodland Scenics are worthy of note, but there are many others.

The key thing to check in N gauge is the finesse of the scatter product. Like ballasting, once you shrink real grass down to N gauge proportions, you would need a microscope to see it. Therefore, adding grass means finding a material that does not make blades of grass look like oak leaves. At one time, most scatter materials were simply made by dyeing sawdust. Some scatter materials are basically foam that is dyed green and then ground up as finely as possible. This type may be more suited to the larger scales. Remember that when you are 'playing trains', the background scenery will be just that, so a blanket of green may suffice.

Once all the formers are in place to define the contours of the landscape, they need to be joined together to form a base for the top of the scenery. Strips of thin cardboard (from food packaging, such as cereal packets) are first glued horizontally between the formers, as seen on the left. When the glue has dried, more strips are added but this time vertically and woven through the horizontal strips. The resulting weave is already quite strong, even before the top layers are added.

With all of the weave completed for the scenic contours, the surface for the road can be added. First, the cardboard foundation is sealed with PVA and then coated with a filler. Almost any kind of filler will do, such as plaster, gap filler, even tile cement. Many of the 'ready-mixed' types are ideal and quick to use. Add several thin layers of filler and allow to dry thoroughly between applications, since this avoids cracks as it dries.

After the final layer for the road has dried, sand it in order to remove any odd bumps or marks made by the application tools. If necessary, fill in any divots and sand again. Then the road can be painted, a light grey being the most appropriate colour, especially for pre-war road surfaces as on Tunley Marsh.

After finishing the road surface it is time to cover the cardboard weave. The quickest and cheapest method is shown here, namely papier mâché using newspaper and PVA. Start with thin rectangular strips at the edges as this makes it easier to butt up to the edges of the back scene and the road. Then infill with overlapping pieces between the edges as shown above the road. Use triangular pieces for the infill as this is a shape that will better mould itself to the contours of the formers and the weave.

After all the papier mâché work is done and the glue has thoroughly dried, it is a good idea to paint the scenery with some kind of 'earth' colour. Cheap poster paints for children's art are ideal. Although the papier mâché will ultimately be covered by scenic scatter materials, any bald spots where the scatter material may come unstuck in the future will otherwise stand out.

It helps the illusion if there is a hint of distant hills, otherwise the scenery will meet the 'sky' rather abruptly. Prior to fitting, the back scene was painted with light blue emulsion using a roller and then clouds were stippled on with white emulsion (this avoids obvious brush strokes). You do not need to be an artist to paint some hills. These ones were done with acrylics (just brown and green and some water to vary the shades) and once the foreground details are completed and trees added, the impressionistic effect will help to blend the three-dimensional to the two-dimensional.

Most of the tools for applying scatter materials are the same as for ballasting, with just the addition of brushes for spreading glue over larger areas. Always buy a selection of green scatters (seen at the top), as nature is never a uniform shade of green. Reuse food containers that have lids (seen in the centre) to store scatters, as they are much easier to use than reaching into plastic bags. The Noch puffer bottle on the left is a simple means of applying very short static grass fibres (seen top left) without the expense of buying a machine to create a static charge.

Most scenic materials can be applied in much the same way as ballasting, using a water and glue mix with a dash of washing-up liquid. Ballast is on the level but hills are not, so much of the scatter material can simply roll away. Therefore, an alternative is to first apply a white glue, such as woodworking glue or PVA. Apply the glue quite thickly, then scatter the scenic material over the glue (hence, why scenic material is often called 'scatter material'). Don't worry too much about perfect coverage at this stage, as any bald spots can be treated again later once the glue has dried.

If you want grass to look like grass (lots of blades reaching for the sky), especially if you are trying to represent something wild and overgrown rather than

Adding scatter materials to the flat parts of the layout is just the same as ballasting. Start by adding a fairly cheap green scatter to the flat area (seen here working leftwards from the bridge); this gives a basic cover. The cheaper 'sawdust'-type scatters are fine for this step, and any basic 'green' colour will suffice, as the idea is to provide a base layer, a bit like a painter applying an undercoat.

Add some other green scatter materials, preferably slightly better quality ones, on to the base carpet of basic green. Pinch a small amount of scatter between thumb and forefinger and then rub your fingers over the area to be covered. It's just like sprinkling a pinch of salt while cooking, and like cooking, it stops you adding too much. Don't aim to cover the base scatter; the tonal variations between light and mid-greens is more realistic than the uniformity of the same colour.

The more different scatter materials you can apply, the better, since Mother Nature has many shades of green. Here, some dark greens, and even a touch of brown, have been added, as well as a smidgen of multi-coloured scatter (reds and yellows) to represent a few wild flowers.

With all the various scatter materials in place, it's time to fix them permanently. Just as with ballasting, the first step is to wet the scatter with a fine mist from a sprayer. Old T-shirts and towels have been placed around the area being worked on to prevent overspray from wetting other areas of already completed scenery. This is particularly important for any scenic features, such as buildings that are made from card, as wetting them may cause them to warp.

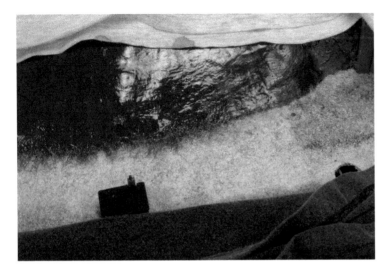

The glue used is a fifty–fifty mix of PVA and water with a drop of washing-up liquid to reduce the surface tension. Hold an eye-dropper just above the wetted scatter and apply just enough until the scatter appears mostly white with glue. Don't be afraid to add a touch of black poster paint to the glue to turn it off-white or light grey. Some scatter materials can be a very vivid colour, and the poster paint helps to just tone things down a little to a more natural shade. Leave the glue to dry overnight and don't be tempted to touch it to see if it is dry, even if the whiteness soon disappears.

The next day, the glue has dried and the scatter materials are securely held to the layout. A different approach is now needed to complete this section as gravity means that the scenic materials simply slide off the slope between the two levels.

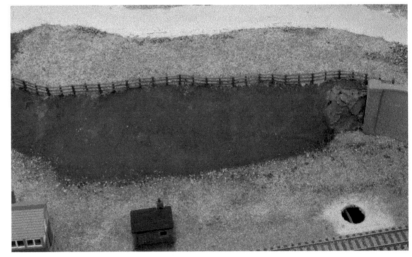

In order to fix the scatter materials to the slope, the first step is to give it a liberal coating of PVA glue (not diluted with water). Quite a large area can be worked as the glue takes a while to dry.

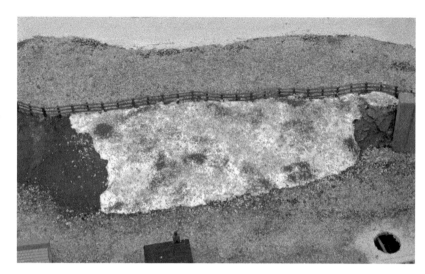

It's simply a case of spreading the scatter materials over the glue, once again using a selection of different products and shades for variety. This view is halfway through the application. If there are any thin patches or bald spots, once the glue has dried, it is easy to add some more glue and scatter.

One of the problems with applying scatter materials to a slope by sprinkling them on is that it can be difficult to get them into every nook and cranny. This puffer bottle from Noch, used in conjunction with their short-fibre scatter material, quickly and completely covers a large area. In addition, shaking the bottle first will statically charge the fibres so that they 'stand up' as they hit the glue. This gives a realistic and even tactile finish.

Inevitably, a lot of scatter material ends up where it shouldn't be, such as here, where green material can be seen on the coaling stage and the track. As no glue has been applied in these places, the scatters remain loose. Any type of vacuum cleaner will remove them but this is potentially quite wasteful. Using the type that collects into a container means that the scatter material is easily recovered – simply empty it on to a sheet of paper and then reuse it on the layout. Do make sure that the vacuum cleaner has itself been scrupulously cleaned of whatever was previously sucked up to avoid contaminating the scatter materials with dust and debris, and only perform this task once all the glue has thoroughly dried.

a regularly mown lawn, you need to use grass fibres rather than scatter material. Grass fibres are very thin fibres that come in differing lengths. The difficulty, until recently, has been to get them to stand up and not look like they have been trampled down by a herd of cows. The key factor with these fibres is that they can be attracted by static electricity. The preparation is the same as for scatter, with white glue being spread over the area to be treated. A cheap application, which works on short- and medium-length fibres, is to 'blow' them onto the glue from a plastic 'puffer bottle'.

For perfect results every time, and to be able to apply longer fibres, you need the Noch Gras-Master. Although it is expensive to buy (the price of a couple of locomotives), if you have a large amount of rural scenery to complete, it will be a wise investment, to acheive top-quality grass effects. The grass fibres receive an electrostatic charge, so that when they land on the glue, they land vertically.

If using electrostatic grass-fibres sounds too complicated, you can buy 'grass mats', which are big enough to represent several large fields in N gauge. Whatever method you choose, one of the key tricks is to avoid buying all the same colour of grass material. Mother Nature is green, but closer inspection will reveal that it is all shades of green. Therefore, while one grass material may dominate your rural scene, do buy several other different packets, and mix and match a bit to get a more realistic tonal variety.

HEDGES AND TREES

An old favourite for hedges is to cut pan scourers into strips. These can seem a little coarse for N gauge, unless heavily treated with additional scatter material. They will also have the regimented shape of a garden hedge, rather than the slightly more random shape of a country lane hedge. A healthy hedge is just a green wall, so any internal former, such as a strip of balsa wood, will do once it is covered in scatter. Remember to paint the balsa wood brown in case you get any bald spots in the future.

Trees are a different matter, as they come in all shapes and sizes, even within the same species. Model railways tend to be set in summer, so the trees are

green, regardless of whether they are deciduous or evergreen. Trees are also surprisingly big things in real life and there is a tendency to model trees smaller than they should be. Real trees would tower over a locomotive, yet in model form this somehow seems out of proportion, especially if you are just modelling a few trees and not a forest.

There are many ways to make your own trees, usually by joining and then unfurling several spliced cables, to form an armature. To this can be fixed light foam or even lichens to form a basic canopy, which can be greatly enhanced by adding green scatter materials. Slightly easier is to use 'tree kits', which come with moulded plastic armatures and all the materials to represent the leaves.

Fortunately, there are some extremely good ready-made trees available for N gauge, though unsurprisingly they are not cheap. If you only require a handful of well-made trees for a largely open rural scene, investing in a few of these trees is cost-effective and

These trees were obtained quite cheaply from the Far East via a supplier on eBay. They illustrate how you can make a tree from stranded electrical cable, which is unfurled to produce branches as you progress up the tree. You can just make out the twisted nature of the strands of the cable in the trunk. While these models do not represent any specific kind of tree, they are sufficiently cheap and 'tree-like' for filling the gaps towards the rear of a layout.

Trees in the Bachmann Scenecraft range are much more expensive but you get what you pay for. These sycamore trees have proper trunks, better branches and much finer foliage. You can use the slightly crude plastic 'root' bases, but they do detach if you want to actually 'plant' your tree in the scenery. While a forest of these model trees would be prohibitively expensive, use a few near the front of a layout for real visual impact.

time-saving. If you need a heavily wooded area or a forest, you need to explore other options. When looking at densely planted areas of healthy trees, you only really see the tops of the trees once you get beyond the initial tree line. You can use ready-made trees for the tree line and beyond that, what are called 'puffball' trees, which are balls of foam with scatter material on top to represent the top of a forest canopy.

Many different ready-made trees are available in N gauge from the likes of Noch, Woodland Scenics and Bachmann Scenescape. The Continental manufacturers like Noch have the largest ranges, and not just the coniferous type trees of the alpine regions that are often modelled.

DOWN ON THE FARM

A farm scene is very popular for anyone modelling a railway in a rural location. Farmers were good customers for the railways, so it is not unreasonable to have a farm close to a station, many of which had a cattle dock for transporting livestock. There is a good range of products available in N gauge to represent all or part of a farm, with a number of suitable cameo scenes.

Any decent-sized model house will do for a farmhouse but Kestrel specifically make a kit for one, as well as a stable block, cow shed and barn. Bachmann Scenecraft produce ready-made farm buildings. There are plenty of model tractors covering the introduction of mechanization to the present day; of particular note are some of the Continental models that are available, such as from Busch. If you are modelling a pre-mechanization scene, you can even get N gauge shire horses.

Livestock is widely available, from pigs to sheep and cows. There are white-metal models, which can vary in quality and need painting, all the way through to finely moulded ready-painted plastic ones from Continental suppliers. Remember that the difference in scale between British N gauge and Continental N gauge will not be discernible for something like the size of a cow.

Fields can be modelled using the same methods for applying scenic materials as for hills. The boundaries of fields can be marked with dry-stone walls, for which there are some excellent products, such as those from Ancorton Models. There are also fencing products for N gauge; of particular note is the flexible fencing from Peco, which can follow the contours of the landscape.

The farmhouse in the Bachmann Scenecraft range is typical of the ready-made resin buildings that are now widely available. Some can be a little crude in places or badly finished, so check them carefully before buying. This example is outstanding for both its level of detail and finish.

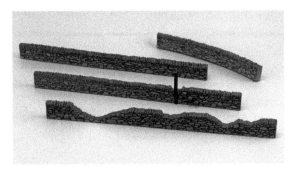

Dry-stone walling is characteristic of so many rural and farming areas in Britain, and there are several products available in N gauge. Probably the best and the most flexible is that from Ancorton Models, with a range including straight, curved, straight with stile and 'ruined'.

The farmyard can be developed in situ on the baseboard, but one final idea is to model the scene as a separate diorama on its own base. This allows easy all-round access to the scene at the comfort of your workbench. Once completed, the whole scene can be installed onto the layout and the edges blended with the surroundings; this is easier if those edges are the boundary walls.

CANALS

You may be surprised to find a section on canals in a book about model railways, yet they are an ever-popular scene on model railways because in real life, the railways often followed the same course as the

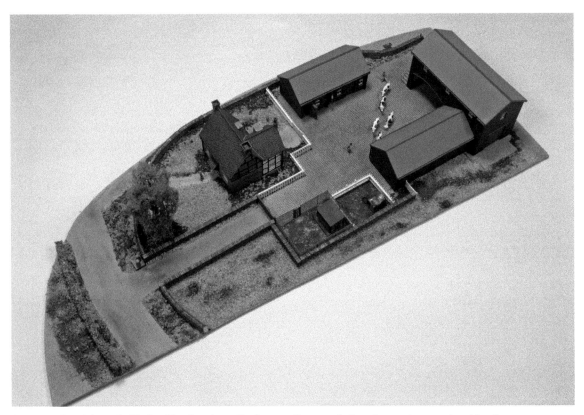

The completed farm for Tunley Marsh, using a Bachmann Scenecraft farm house, barn and stables from Kestrel, and dry-stone walls by Ancorton Models. Note how the entire scene has been built on a thin piece of hardboard so that it could be worked on away from the layout. Some of the edges are left bare so that they can be blended into the layout when the scene is finally installed. When adding small details in N gauge, such as the people and animals, it can be easier if the scene can be worked on at a table, especially if it is for the rear of a layout where access may be difficult.

Canals and railways are often found together, so they make for interesting scenes on a model railway. Just like railways, canals still require quite a bit of infrastructure so N gauge gives you the space to realistically represent them. This is a superb scene on Kinlet Wharf by the Wyre Forest Model Railway Club with a narrow boat emerging from under a substantial girder bridge, which carries the railway tracks. There is just enough reflection from the canal surface for it to realistically look like water.

canals, which preceded them. Like the railways, canals were built to join population centres for the transport of goods, so they can be found in gritty urban environments or a bucolic countryside setting.

Canals are long and thin, like railways, but they can still take up a lot of space and require substantial infrastructure. If you model a junction or a canal basin, you need to represent a surprising amount of water in order to turn a full-length narrow boat. Perhaps for this reason, canals seem to be more popular on N gauge layouts than in any other scale.

Hornby's Lyddle End range includes some ready-made canal sections, including locks that can be joined together, as required – a bit like sectional track. They also, understandably, make canal boats, as do Langley Models who also make lock gates and transfers for the boats. If modelling a lock, it will be necessary to have the canal on two different levels, either by raising one section above the baseboard, or sinking another section into the baseboard. This is another example of where the open-frame baseboard may be beneficial.

Canals and railways often cross and any of the railway-bridging solutions will be appropriate. Canals sometimes enter tunnels too, though N gauge portals will be far too large; however, by stepping down a scale to Z gauge, there are tunnel mouths that would be just the right size.

WATER

Like canals, water is a very popular subject for inclusion on a model railway. It's often just another excuse to have an impressive bridge structure; real railways try to avoid large bodies of water, as they require yet more expensive infrastructure. Water can be one of the hardest things to get right on a model. Don't be tempted to use real water. Apart from the fact that it's wet and gets everywhere, tap water is just too clear to represent anything but the purest of mountain streams.

The still waters of a canal, slow-moving river or dock are traditionally represented with layers of varnish, and do not require any great physical depth for the scene. Prepare the base by painting with browns and greens, depending on how murky you want your water to be. For wider rivers, use dark tones in the middle for depth and lighter tones by the edges. Then apply numerous coats of gloss varnish; you may literally require dozens. The idea is to keep adding another coat until the 'water' develops a visual depth that looks like water. Use a good-quality varnish and apply thinly; don't be tempted to speed things up with thick layers, as this can lead to white patches where the varnish does not dry properly. Also, be careful to avoid obvious brush strokes in the varnish – don't brush in straight lines, as any lines from curving strokes can always be regarded as slight ripples.

Varnish for water can still lack depth, and is no good if you want to have rocks in the water or any kind of detritus like an old bicycle. For this you need one of the casting resin waters. Preparation starts with painting, as before, but you need to make sure that your base is totally sealed or the resin will leak out. Most of the casting resins are of two parts, which need to be carefully measured and mixed together. The mix can then be gently poured into the base. The baseboard must be level, or you could end up with water flowing uphill. For fast-flowing water, once the resin is partially cured, it is possible to lightly scribe ripples into the surface before it fully hardens. Then leave it to properly cure and you should end up with very realistic-looking water.

SHIPS AND BOATS

One final water-related section on scenery concerns ships and boats. Goods were often interchanged between rail and water at ports and docks of varying sizes. A surprising number of N gauge boat models are available, such as the TID tug and paddle steamer from Langley Models. They also make a Clyde Puffer, as do Gramodels, a prototype that is ideal for a small rail and water interchange.

A number of American manufacturers make small boats and tugs that are suitable for British N gauge layouts. Although hard to find now, look out for some of the Revell ship kits – these were made to a scale of 1:144, almost perfect for British N gauge.

N Gauge is surprisingly well served for models of ships and boats, probably more so than the larger scales. Boats, and especially ships, are surprisingly large things, so you need quite a bit of space for them, for which N gauge is ideal. The full hull model on the left is a TID Tug by Langley Models, while the Clyde Puffer on the right is a waterline model by Gramodels.

BACK SCENES

You cannot avoid having a rear to your layout because, unlike the real world, it cannot go on forever. Avoid having no back scene at all, since all you will see is a wall behind, which destroys any illusion you have worked hard for your N gauge layout to create. The easiest back scene is simply a representation of the sky. This works well in a rural scene, possibly with the hills rising to the rear of the layout. It can fail to convince in a more urban setting, where you glimpse clear blue sky between the buildings, when there should be other buildings instead.

If you are a reasonable artist, you can paint your own back scene. Paint buildings on the back scene proportionally reduced in size to suggest that they are in the distance. Try continuing roads from the front to the rear of the layout, gradually narrowing the road on the baseboard, and continuing to narrow the road as it is painted on to the back scene. Be aware, though, that this is a very difficult trick to pull off convincingly. Sometimes, it only looks right when looking straight at it, and as you move to either side it fails to convince.

Painted back scenes printed on to thin paper have been available to modellers for years; however,

although many are sold as suitable for any gauge, some of the urban settings are just too big for N gauge. General rural scenes without any man-made objects are suitable for N gauge, no matter what scale they are intended for.

Realistic photographic back scenes are now widely available and becoming increasingly popular. If you are comfortable with digital photography and a computer, you can soon create your own. Photographic back scenes can work very well but they can sometimes be too realistic. Digital photography and printing allow for the presentation of a high level of detail but it can be difficult to model an equivalent level of detail in the foreground, especially in N gauge. This inconsistency means that you are looking at two very different levels of presentation that will make the back scene stand out, when you really want it to blend in.

A painted back scene, even if you are no artist, can be made to look a little more 'impressionist', and a 'soft and fuzzy' background is less noticeable. It is out of focus, which tricks the eye into thinking that it is further away than it really is. A pin-sharp digital image will not achieve that trick. Despite all this caution, there are some very good 'generic' photo back scenes available at reasonable prices and they are well worth a look.

A good back scene makes it appear as though the layout goes on beyond the boundaries of the base-board. This view into the far corner of Imperial Yard by Pete Latham has images of buildings and trees on the back scene, which makes the depth of the layout appear to be much greater.

CHAPTER ELEVEN

BRING YOUR LAYOUT TO LIFE

They say that the devil is in the detail. While a model railway can have swathes of track, sweeping hills and impressive buildings, it's the little details that will actually bring your layout to life. You only need to look around you in the real world: there are people, cars, telegraph poles, road signs, street names and so much more. We tend to take these things for granted simply because they are everyday objects. If you take them away, you'll have that feeling that something is missing. If they are not there on your model railway, you will also have a feeling that something is missing.

Take a moment to look around you and try to absorb all the little details, big and small, that give a place its character and atmosphere. This is easy to do if you are modelling the contemporary scene. What do you do if you want to model a time and place in the past? Your memory may be an uncertain friend, but there are many books and photographs to help. Like stepping into a time-machine, you can enter the black and white world of the past by studying the thousands of photographs to be found in books and on the internet. There are lots of books about trains for reference material, some of which include details beyond the boundary fence of the railway; where you need more details, look for the many books published on all aspects of 'times gone by'.

There are many sayings, and quite a few just in the world of model railways. Perhaps the most often-quoted saying is that 'a model railway layout is never finished'. This alludes to there always being some additional small details that you can add, and keep adding, no matter how old your layout is. The real world is a very detailed place and your N gauge model railway can be just the same.

MODEL PEOPLE

A model railway without model people will look like a ghost town. The trick is to get the balance right, depending on the scene. A busy city terminus will have

Continental manufacturers produce a range of astonishingly detailed figures, such as these from Noch. Most of them will be suitable for any era from the early twentieth century all the way up to the present day.

up to a hundred staff and passengers milling around the concourse and platforms. That number of bodies at a small branch-line station will look very odd, unless it is market day, but market day only comes once a week.

There is a wide range of little people for N gauge and an equally wide variation in quality. P&D Marsh and Langley Models produce many figures cast in white metal; the quality of white-metal casting is never as good as moulded plastic, but these figures are more than acceptable, although you do have to paint them yourself. The softness of white metal does mean that a small amount of anatomical repositioning is possible for added variety.

If you need a crowd scene and you don't mind painting figures, there are some cheap bargain packs that can be ordered direct from the Far East via the internet. In N gauge, no one is ever going to see the whites of their eyes, so dabs of colour for face, hair, hands and clothes are acceptable, especially if the figures are going to be towards the rear of the layout and thus furthest away from the viewer.

Where figures can clearly be seen in the foreground, it is worth investing in ready-painted plastic figures. Bachmann Scenecraft have recently introduced these figures for British layouts, but prior to that, it was once again a case of looking towards the Continental market for quality and variety, particularly the figures from Preiser and Noch. Passengers and workmen are largely the same around the world, so these Continental figures are quite at home on British layouts, allowing for the period being modelled. Uniformed figures, such as station staff or policemen, are a different matter, as uniform styles tend to be more specific to each country. You could do a little repainting but that defeats the object of paying top price for quality figures.

Passengers are not just useful for stations. There is a tendency to run model coaches without any passengers on board. You can buy seated passengers but not all coaching stock interiors will accommodate the legs. The simplest option is a pack of cheap, unpainted figures, either standing or seated. Paint them above the waistline and then cut them in half, attaching the torso upwards into coach seating, as you will never be able to tell that the legs are missing.

Some road vehicles are instantly recognizable as much as some trains and sometimes just as iconic, so decent models are essential for modellers. Here are taxis old and new from Oxford Diecast; the 'London Black Cab' on the right is indispensable for any town or city station forecourt from the 1960s to the present day.

ROAD VEHICLES

Most model railway layouts will feature at least one road, even if it is just an excuse for an over-bridge or a level crossing. If you have modelled a station, it will require road access or else passengers and goods will not be able to get to the trains. If you have roads, it stands to reason that you will want to have some road vehicles on them.

While you may know precisely the suitability or otherwise of a locomotive for a period depicted on a layout, modellers are generally a bit hazier about the

The horse was the main means of motive power on roads for longer than you might think. On the left is a white metal kit for a delivery cart from Langley Models, which would have been seen all over the country, but especially towns and cities. On the right is a simple two-wheel cart, in this case as a milk float, also in white metal but produced by Knightwing.

At one time, you could only get N gauge UK road vehicles as white metal kits, such as this selection from Langley Models and P&D Marsh. Solid-cast cabs mean that the windows cannot be see-through; however, using shiny paints, such as silver, means that some of the reflective properties of glass can at least be simulated, as seen with the windscreen of the vehicle on the far right.

correct period for road vehicles. The horse was king for longer than you might think, and cars were owned by the few, in complete contrast to today. There is a temptation to collect road vehicles as much as railway rolling stock, but crowded country roads in a rural setting are only a recent phenomenon.

For many years, Langley Models and P&D Marsh have supported N gauge with a range of simple white metal kits for road vehicles, from horse-drawn carts to cars and lorries. As most modellers used to represent scenes prior to the 1960s, this tended to influence the range of vehicles that was produced. Those looking to model the present day had to look elsewhere.

Most modern-era car designs are sold across Europe, and so are as at home in Britain as on the Continent. There has always been a good range of Continental models available, such as those from Wiking, but two obvious problems present themselves for the British N gauge modeller. First, if the steering wheel is modelled, then it is on the wrong side. This is only a major problem if you are close enough to discern this detail, and you can always park the car facing away from you. The second problem is one of scale – Continental N Gauge, being 1:160 instead of British 1:148, is smaller and it seems noticeably so when using Continental-manufactured model cars.

You can get away with using the Continental models in a 1:148 setting with care. Do not mix British and Continental models, as the size difference will be immediately obvious. If you do want models from both sources, keep them well separated in different scenes on the layout. Try to keep the Continental models towards the rear of the layout; for example, have a road that runs along the back scene. By making the road slightly narrower as well, you get forced perspective, which makes the layout seem deeper than it actually is.

A more recent source for modern N gauge road vehicles has been the Japanese collectors' market,

The range of Japanese limited-edition road vehicles from Tomytec is perfect for British modellers, as they are the correct scale, the steering wheel is on the right and they are easily disassembled for alteration or repainting. The model on the left is straight out of the box – the green number plate and Japanese writing are easily anglicized with a bit of paint. The model on the right has been thus treated, as well as replacing the box superstructure with a flatbed.

The ever-expanding range of ready-made road vehicles from Oxford Diecast has been hugely popular with N gauge modellers in the last few years. While the focus is mainly on the most popular railway modelling period of the 1950s and 1960s, the accuracy, finish and reasonable price of the models have made them much sought after.

mainly the products of Tomytec. These models are sold as limited editions for people to collect, but they are hugely popular with British N gauge modellers and with good reason. Japanese N gauge is a scale of 1:150, which is nearly identical to the British scale of 1:148 and, of course, the Japanese also drive on the left. Some of the models look more 'foreign' than others, so you have to choose carefully; however, if you do not mind a bit of alteration and some repainting (mainly the lorries and buses), you can soon have a

highly detailed road vehicle for your modern N gauge layout.

It is also possible to buy packs of cheap plastic car models directly from the Far East via the internet. These are of variable quality and scale; however, if you require a lot of cars for a particular application, they are a simple and affordable option. For example, where cars are densely packed into a car park or nose-to-tail in a traffic jam, it's more about sheer impact of numbers than minor details of the vehicles.

Articulated lorries are a necessary scenic road feature for any layout set in the last thirty years, particularly around industrial areas. There are many sources of models but a mishmash of scales. From left to right can be seen products from Wiking (Continental 1:160), Intertrans 148 (correct scale 1:148 for N gauge; distributed by Graham Farish but no longer available) and Tomytec (Japanese 1:150 scale). The difference in scale between the Wiking lorry and the others is subtle but still apparent.

If you are modelling a goods yard, you need small trucks to deliver and remove all the goods that the railway transports. The two Leyland trucks on the left are made by Base Toys, while the British Railways horsebox is an Oxford Diecast product.

Buses have been the competition for railways for many years, and they brought about the demise of many rail routes; however, their increasing ubiquity is all the more reason to include them on model railway layouts. Many bus models are available in N gauge, such as these double-decker classics. The Routemaster bus on the left is made by Oxford Diecast, while the Leyland Atlantean on the right is a Graham Farish by Bachmann model.

Like buses, coaches have provided damaging competition to the railways over the years. These N gauge Oxford Diecast models represent the oldest and the newest in road coaches.

Once again, though, do not be tempted to mix and match with superior quality models, as the latter will stand out from a sea of nondescript models.

The expansion of new N gauge products for UK modellers has not just been limited to the railway rolling stock. Several manufacturers, mainly Oxford Diecast, Base Toys and Graham Farish by Bachmann, have introduced a wide range of good-quality, very affordable road vehicles that are generally the correct scale for N gauge.

SIGNAGE

What would we do without signs to tell us where to go and adverts to tell us what to buy? Signage and its design can set the time and sometimes the place very quickly. Black and white cast road signs pointing this way and that at road junctions instantly evoke a pre-war rural idyll, as much as a big blue motorway sign suggests the modernity of the 1960s onwards. You would not expect to see a road junction without a give way sign, and it should be the same for a model railway. There are several very impressive collections of ready-made modern road signs, such as those from Ancorton Models.

Advertising in public is not a new idea. A characteristic of old stations was the tinplate adverts for everything from OXO to Guinness and these are available on a printed sheet from several manufacturers, such as Langley Models. Simply cut out a selection and stick them around your layout. Larger hoardings are available from Trackside Signs and Ten Commandments.

LEFT: *This period road sign warning of a left-hand curve in the road ahead is an exquisite ready-painted detail item for N gauge, which is available from Ancorton Models.*

BELOW: *Steam-era stations would have been awash with tinplate advertising signs and also advertising posters for the railway company itself. These self-adhesive poster boards for the GWR are made by Tiny Signs; the images and text are clearly visible, albeit with the aid of a magnifying glass.*

Advertising wherever you go is not a new phenomenon. The railways have always advertised themselves and advertised other products on their premises. These hoardings are available in N gauge from Trackside Signs as either sheets for the modeller to cut and mount or individually and already mounted on a hoarding.

STREET FURNITURE

The slightly curious phrase 'street furniture' is given to anything that you might find along a street, of which there is a surprising amount that you might take for granted. This includes post boxes, telephone boxes, benches, street lights, grids, manhole covers, bus stops, traffic lights (and crossings) and signs. Once again, the design and style of these items can determine the period in which they are set. Many were made from solid cast iron, which gave them a very long life indeed. You can still find the odd post box with 'GR' on it rather than 'ER'.

There is a good selection of street furniture items available from manufacturers such as Langley Models and P&D Marsh. These tend to be either white-metal castings or etched brass. Many of the former are one-piece castings, which simply need to be painted.

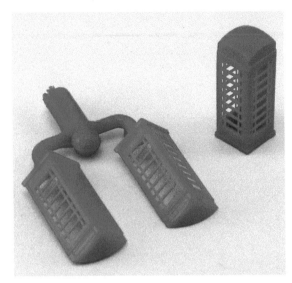

Peco make the classic Gilbert Scott designed telephone box as a very simple kit of two triangular-shaped halves that simply clip together without the need for glue. There once was a time when telephone boxes were seen everywhere, and every station had at least one outside.

This pre-war scene on Tunley Marsh illustrates how a few items of so-called 'street furniture' can add interesting and realistic detail to a scene in N gauge. The post box and telephone box are plastic kits from Peco, the gas lamp is a white metal item from P&D Marsh and the delicate spear point railings are produced in plastic by Ratio.

Even if there are a few parts, they are easily constructed with superglue. Etched brass can be a little more challenging – superglue will again hold everything together, but they often have delicate parts that require removal from a fret and sometimes a degree of bending to shape. Peco have recently introduced some pre-coloured plastic items, such as telephone boxes and post boxes, which need little more than separating from a sprue and installing on your layout.

BOXES, BARRELS AND CRATES

Railways are all about moving things. Before the advent of containerization and the pallet, everything was transported in crates, boxes and barrels. It would be usual to see such items scattered around goods yards and at the customer's site (such as a factory). Many other things can be seen as well – pipes, oil drums, lengths of timber and steel section.

Many manufacturers make these details of goods in transit, such as P&D Marsh, but particular mention should be made of the range from Ten Commandments. As with many of the items that are available, a lot of the range is sold as loads for open wagons, but most are perfectly suitable for placing into a corner of a goods yard or factory. Virtually all of these accessories need painting but this allows for a degree of customization and variety – you can use the same load many times, even in the same place, but a mixture of colours avoids the obvious appearance of repetition.

Many of the range of wagon loads, such as these boxes, barrels and crates from Ten Commandments, look just as good placed around a goods yard or factory.

CAMEO SCENES

The many cameo scenes that it is possible to model fall into the 'love them or hate them' category with railway modellers. Some modellers feel that a cameo scene is by definition clichéd and unoriginal, and is thus to be avoided at all costs. At the end of the day, it is your model railway, and not someone else's. If you want to include a cameo scene because it amuses you or means something to you, then there is no one to stop you.

Some of the most popular cameo scenes revolve around churches. There are some very good kits for churches from Kestrel and Metcalfe Models. A church is quite a large building and will require a large footprint to be modelled in its entirety with its surroundings. It's quite feasible to model just a portion of a church in low relief at the back of a layout. The architecture of churches is sufficiently distinctive that only a portion needs to be modelled to instantly see what it is. The typical cameo scene is a wedding, with bride and groom and guests outside for photographs. By the roadside, the cars (or horse and carriage) can be modelled. For those with more macabre tastes, a funeral scene can be modelled. You can make an easy start with either scene by purchasing the relevant detail set from Langley Models.

Another popular cameo scene (for some unknown reason) is the road crash. Typically this shows a car that has veered off the road, perhaps damaging some fencing in the process. Like road works, this is an excuse for queues of traffic, as well as the attendant emergency services with police cars, ambulances and fire engines. All the vehicles and people you need are available, so possibly it is this easy availability that explains the popularity.

The most effective cameo scenes are the ones that are the simplest in their construction. They should not be so overly elaborate that they detract the eye from the trains. This scene on a loading dock contains just one figure and a selection of crates. The man is sitting down but looking in a particular direction, perhaps waiting for someone to help him move the crates.

Implied movement is difficult to achieve successfully with a cameo scene. Figures that are posed in the middle of some strenuous activity, such as swinging a pickaxe, can look a little odd as they are permanently frozen in position while trains are moving around them. In this scene, the movement is subtle as the woman comes from the house to collect groceries being delivered by the man.

Everyone hates road works, yet with amusing irony, it's a scene that modellers love to recreate on their layouts. Perhaps modellers believe that going by train is still a better way to travel than by road. It's an interesting excuse to have a queue of road vehicles on what might otherwise be a quiet road. The machinery of road works from steam rollers to modern tracked diggers can be found, with some exquisite examples from the American, Japanese and Continental manufacturers. The ubiquitous traffic cone is available from the likes of P&D Marsh, and you can even get them ready painted.

There are many figures to be found that are wielding pickaxes or shovels. It is a simple matter to cut a small hole or trench in the baseboard to give the impression of a repair to a gas or water main. There are several manufacturers of the universal skip, which can be found anywhere and everywhere these days, with P&D Marsh also making a skip lorry. For larger works, you can get portacabins and security fencing.

Beyond these popular scenes on a model railway, a cameo scene can be as simple or as complex as you wish. A simple scene could be a couple of people

There is implied movement in this cameo scene, which could equally be no movement. The standing worker is instructing the fork-lift truck driver to stop where he is. The scene is finished by numerous small details, such as the oil drums, pallets, sacks and the ubiquitous traffic cones.

chatting outside a Post Office, or children playing in a street. A complex scene could be a market day in full swing in a town centre with lots of stalls and people. All cameo scenes are realistic, and are fully appropriate on a model railway layout that seeks to achieve realism. The trick is not to overdo things such that one scene dominates the layout, or that too many scenes start to make the layout seem to be unrealistically busy. Above all, cameo scenes can be fun, which is what building an N gauge layout is all about.

USEFUL CONTACTS

2mm Scale Association
24 Hillsborough Terrace, York YO30 6EW
www.2mm.org.uk
Voluntary organization that promotes and facilitates
modelling at the scale of 2mm:1ft via advice from
members and exclusive components.

BH Enterprises
68 Meadow Road, Kingswood, Garston,
Hertfordshire WD25 0JA
Tel: 01923 672809
www.bh-enterprises.co.uk
Manufacturer of white metal and plastic model railway kits, scenic items and accessories.

C=Rail Intermodal
'Morven' Roome Bay Avenue, Crail, Fife KY10 3TR
Tel: 01333 450976
www.c-rail-intermodal.co.uk
Manufacturer of high-quality plastic kits and transfers
for ISO containers.

Dapol
Gledrid Industrial Park, Chirk, Wrexham LL14 5DG
Tel: 01691 774455
www.dapol.co.uk
Manufacturer of ready-to-run locomotives, coaches,
wagons and train sets.

Dornaplas
2 Springside Cottages, Dornafield Road, Ipplepen,
Newton Abbot, Devon TQ12 5SJ
Tel: 01803 813749
www.springsidemodels.com
Manufacturer of plastic kits for buildings and road
vehicles.

Etched Pixels
Etched Pixels Digital Design, 106 Walter Road,
Swansea, SA1 5QQ
www.etchedpixels.co.uk
Manufacturer of etched-brass rolling stock kits and
white metal details.

Fleetline Road 'n' Rail
Lytchett Manor Models, 48 Woolavington Road,
Puriton, Bridgewater, Somerset TA7 8BQ
Tel: 01278 685302
www.lytchettmanor.co.uk
Manufacturer of white metal kits, scenic accessories
and details.

Gaugemaster Controls Ltd
Gaugemaster House, Ford Road, Arundel, West
Sussex BN18 0BN
Tel: 01903 884488
www.gaugemaster.com
Manufacturer of controllers and scenic accessories,
as well as a shop with a comprehensive selection of
models.

Graham Farish by Bachmann
Bachmann Ltd, Moat Way, Barwell, Leicestershire
LE9 8EY
www.bachmann.co.uk
Manufacturer of ready-to-run locomotives, coaches,
wagons and train sets.

Gramodels
18 Lower Tail, Carpenders Park, Watford,
Hertfordshire WD19 5DD
Tel: 07833 364274
www.gramodels.co.uk
Manufacturer of resin kits for military vehicles, wagons and boats.

Kestrel Designs
Gaugemaster House, Ford Road, Arundel, West
Sussex BN18 0BN
Tel: 01903 884488
www.gaugemaster.com
Versatile range of plastic kits for buildings supplied by
Gaugemaster.

Langley Models
166 Three Bridges Road, Crawley, Sussex RH10 1LE
Tel: 01293 516329
www.langleymodels.co.uk
Manufacturer of white metal kits, scenic accessories
and details.

Mathieson Models
135 Carr Lane, York YO26 5HL
Tel: 01904 341689
www.mathiesonmodels.com
Manufacturer of ready-to-run private-owner coal
wagons.

Metcalfe Models & Toys
Bell Busk, Skipton BD23 4DU
Tel: 01729 830072
Manufacturer of die-cut card kits for buildings.

N Gauge Society
28 Cherry Gardens, Trowbridge, BA14 7AU
www.ngaugesociety.com
Voluntary organization that promotes and facilitates
modelling in N gauge via advice from members and
production of exclusive wagon kits and ready-to-run
rolling stock.

Noch
www.noch.de/en
Manufacturer of scenic and landscaping materials for
model railways.

Oxford Diecast
Tel: 02380 248850
www.oxforddiecast.co.uk
Manufacturer of diecast road vehicles, including cars,
buses, coaches and lorries.

P&D Marsh
The Stables, Wakes End Farm, Eversholt, Milton
Keynes, Buckinghamshire MK17 9FB
Tel: 01525 280068
www.pdmarshmodels.com
Manufacturer of white metal kits, scenic accessories
and details, and a range of laser-cut kits for buildings.

Parkside Dundas
Millie Street, Kirkcaldy, Fife, Scotland, KY1 2NL
Tel: 01592 640896
www.parksidedundas.co.uk
Manufacturer of plastic wagon kits.

Peco
Peco Technical Advice Bureau, Underleys, Beer,
Devon EX12 3NA
Tel: 01297 21542
www.peco-uk.com
Manufacturer of track, wagons, kits for buildings and
scenic accessories.

Preiser
www.preiserfiguren.de
Manufacturer of figures and accessories.

Ratio Plastic Models
Ratio House, Mardle Way, Buckfastleigh, Devon
TQ11 0NR
Tel: 01364 642764
www.peco-uk.com
Manufacturer of plastic kits for buildings and signals.

Robbie's Rolling Stock
2 Whites Close, Abergavenny, Monmouthshire
NP7 5HZ
www.robbiesrollingstock.co.uk
Manufacturer of wagon transfers and coach sides,
with a massive range of hand-finished private-owner
wagons.

Shire Scenes
The Old Armoury, North Street, Somerton,
Somerset, TA11 7NY
Tel: 01458 272 446

www.shirescenes.com
Manufacturer of etched brass kits and scenic items.

Springside Models
2 Springside Cottages, Dornafield Road, Ipplepen,
Newton Abbot, Devon TQ12 5SJ
Tel: 01803 813749
www.springsidemodels.com
Manufacturer of white metal kits and details.

Taylor Precision Models
www.tpmodels.co.uk
Manufacturer of plastic wagon kits and rolling stock
detailing parts.

Ten Commandments
20 Struan Drive, Inverkeithing, Fife KY11 1AR
Tel: 01383 410032
www.cast-in-stone.co.uk
Manufacturer of details, wagon loads and low-relief
buildings cast in plaster.

TimeCast
Unit 5E, Centurion Park, Kendal Road, Shrewsbury,
SY1 4EH
Tel: 01743 465676
www.timecastmodels.co.uk
Manufacturer of kits for buildings, mainly for war-
gaming but still suitable for railway modelling.

Ultima Models
Etched Pixels Digital Design, 106 Walter Road,
Swansea, SA1 5QQ
www.ultima-models.co.uk
Manufacturer of etched-brass rolling stock kits and
white metal details for rolling stock.

Union Mills
Unit 5, Union Mills Trading Estate, Isle of Man
IM4 4AB
Tel: 01624 852896
Manufacturer of ready-to-run locomotives.

INDEX